Y0-ABA-136

HIS NAME
BE PRAISED

HIS NAME BE PRAISED

UNDERSTANDING
CHRIST'S MINISTRY
AND MISSION

ALEXANDER B. MORRISON

DESERET
BOOK

Salt Lake City, Utah

© 2002 Alexander B. Morrison

All rights reserved. No part of this book may be reproduced in any form or by any means without permission in writing from the publisher, Deseret Book Company, P. O. Box 30178, Salt Lake City, Utah 84130. This work is not an official publication of The Church of Jesus Christ of Latter-day Saints. The views expressed herein are the responsibility of the author and do not necessarily represent the position of the Church or of Deseret Book Company.

Deseret Book is a registered trademark of Deseret Book Company.

Visit us at www.deseretbook.com

Library of Congress Cataloging-in-Publication Data

Morrison, Alexander B.
  His name be praised : understanding Christ's mission and ministry / Alexander B. Morrison.
    p.   cm.
  Includes bibliographical references and index.
  ISBN 1-57008-768-7 (alk. paper)
    1. Jesus Christ—Person and offices.   2. Church of Jesus Christ of Latter-day Saints—Doctrines.   3. Mormon Church—Doctrines.   I. Title.
    BT203 .M67 2002
    232—dc21   20011006188

Printed in the United States of America   18961-6912
R. R. Donnelly and Sons, Crawfordsville, IN

10   9   8   7   6   5   4   3   2   1

To my beloved, eternal companion, Shirley,
whose love, wisdom, and purity of heart
inspire and exalt me daily

Contents

Contents

PREFACE

Jesus, the very thought of Thee
With sweetness fills my breast;
But sweeter far Thy face to see
And in Thy presence rest.
HYMNS, NO. 141

The telephone rang at our home in Bountiful, Utah, at about 5:00 P.M. on Tuesday, October 3, 2000. My wife answered it.

"It's Michael Watson, for you," she said, handing me the telephone.

Why would the secretary to the First Presidency be calling me, I wondered.

I soon found out.

"President Hinckley wants you to bear your testimony at the Saturday morning session of general conference," Brother Watson informed me.

I thought about what I might say that would be appropriate and eventually turned to a short statement made by Jesus. Intrigued by John the Baptist's testimony of Jesus, two of John's disciples asked the Master where he dwelt. "Come and see," He said. That seemed to represent both an invitation and a challenge to learn more of Him, and it occurred to me that "come and see" speaks to all in our day who wish to find Him and learn His true identity. To do so is the quest of a lifetime, the most noble endeavor of mankind, the only road to true happiness. "Come and see," I decided, would be the theme for my testimony.

The next morning I scratched out a few lines, and delivered them as requested. The text of my remarks, as they were printed in the *Ensign,* November 2000, is as follows:

"Very early in His ministry, two disciples came to Jesus and asked, 'Master, . . . where dwellest thou?' (John 1:38). Jesus' brief yet profound reply, 'Come and see,' provides the basis for my few poor remarks today.

"'Come and see'—come longing to know Him—

and I promise you will find Him and see Him in His true character as the risen, redeeming Savior of the world. 'Come and see,' and you will recognize Him as the Christ of the empty sepulchre, the conqueror of Calvary, who broke the bands of death and rose triumphant from the tomb, to bring immortality to all and eternal life to the faithful. He is the 'lamb without blemish and without spot,' foreordained in His Messianic role 'before the foundation of the world' (1 Peter 1:19–20). He was 'wounded for our transgressions, he was bruised for our iniquities. . . . With his stripes we are healed' (Isaiah 53:5).

"'Come and see,' and in your coming lay your burdens at His feet. Give away all your sins that you might see and know Him (Alma 22:18). 'Come unto me, all ye that labour and are heavy laden,' He said, 'and I will give you rest. Take my yoke upon you, and learn of me; . . . and ye shall find rest unto your souls' (Matthew 11:28–29). Come unto Him, and He will take away your sins and heal your soul, though it be sick with sin. He will replace hatred with love and selfishness with service. He will strengthen your shoulders to better bear your burdens and give you new courage and hope for the journey ahead.

"'Come and see'—and as you do so your eyes will be opened and you will *really* see, perhaps for the first time, who *you* are, and who *He* is. You will come to see yourself as a child of God, of divine parentage, possessed of infinite capacities to grow spiritually and become more like Him. You will come to understand that God 'hath made of one blood all nations of men for to dwell on all the face of the earth' (Acts 17:26) and you will see all men everywhere as your brothers and all women as your sisters, with all that implies in terms of sibling responsibility. You will see that 'He denieth none that come unto Him, black and white, bond and free, male and female; . . . and all are alike unto God' (2 Nephi 26:33).

"'Come and see'—and as you do so you will find His Church—The Church of Jesus Christ of Latter-day Saints. It is a Church directed on earth by living prophets, seers, and revelators, but its head is no mortal man, but Jesus, the Lord God Omnipotent Himself. As you 'come and see,' you will find a happy people—an optimistic and joyful people—who, while struggling to overcome the usual faults and foibles of humanity, yet strive to be better, to do good to all men, to build the city of God wherein all may dwell together in righteousness. As you 'come and see,' you will find a people with a deep and abiding concern for the poor and the needy, a people who reach out a helping hand to aid the widow and orphan, the sick and afflicted, the poor and oppressed. 'Come and see' the fruits of gospel living. Taste them for yourself and you will find them sweet and delicious. As you come to know that 'when ye are in the service of your fellow beings ye are only in the service of your God' (Mosiah 2:17) you will seek to wear out your life in the service of the Master.

"I finish where I began: Jesus' statement 'come and see' provides both an invitation and a promise to all people everywhere. Come to Him; see Him as King of Kings and Lord of Lords; recognize in Him the Great Messiah who will come again with healing in His wings, to set His people free. He will wrap you about in the cloak of His redeeming love and your life will be changed forever.

"Of this I testify, as one of His servants, in the name of Jesus Christ, amen."

A few days after the conference my wife, Shirley, said, "Perhaps you should consider expanding your remarks into a book. That might help others to find Him." I listened carefully. My wife is one of the wisest people I know. She just doesn't give bad advice.

"I'll try," I replied.

This book is the result of that attempt. Readers will quickly ascertain that extensive use is made of the scriptures in recounting the story of Jesus. For obvious reasons, I make no apology for that. But I acknowledge with thanks and admiration the monumental work of Elder James E. Talmage, whose opus, *Jesus the Christ,* remains the standard against which all Latter-day Saint attempts to portray Jesus must be measured.

ACKNOWLEDGMENTS

I am indebted to my dear friends and associates, Elder Marlin K. Jensen, President Jeffrey C. Swinton, and President William O. Nelson, who read the manuscript and made valuable suggestions for correction and addition. Special thanks go also to Afton Ferris, who literally went the extra mile in typing and correcting the manuscript.

Finally, this book is not an official publication of The Church of Jesus Christ of Latter-day Saints. No Church official asked me to write it, and I alone am responsible for errors and omissions in the text. The views and ideas presented herein are my own and do not necessarily represent those of the Church.

CHAPTER ONE

COME AND SEE . . .
THE FOREORDAINED
MESSIAH

'Tis sweet to sing the matchless love
Of Him who left His home above
And came to earth—oh, wondrous plan—
To suffer, bleed, and die for man!
HYMNS, NO. 176

Jesus, the Apostle Peter said, is the "lamb without blemish and without spot: Who verily was fore-ordained before the foundation of the world, but was manifest in these last times for you" (1 Peter 1:19–20). The apostle used the powerful metaphor of the paschal lamb, central to and sacrificed at the Jewish Feast of the Passover, to make the point that Jesus was chosen and ordained, in the councils of heaven before the world was, to be the Redeemer and Savior of God's children. Foreordination "before the foundation of the world" necessarily implies a premortal existence or state, during which Jesus dwelled with the Father prior to His birth and ministry in the flesh.

It is important to note that Jesus was *fore-ordained*, not *predestined*, to be the Savior.

Latter-day Saints fervently disavow the doctrine of predestination as set out in the sixteenth century by John Calvin, the eminent protestant theologian. Calvin believed, erroneously, that human beings do not have free will or moral agency. He preached that God, in His infinite wisdom, had decided at the beginning of time who would be saved and who would be damned, totally irrespective of human merit (see *A History of World Societies*, 1:466–67). This "terrible decree," as even Calvin called it, has no place in it for either agency or effort; in Calvin's view, there is nothing human beings can do to alter what has already been determined regarding their individual salvation. The doctrine of predestination completely disavows the merit or efficacy of good works or personal righteousness. It denies the mercy and justice of God and makes it appear that He is a respecter of persons. Predestination denies the principle that mortality is a probationary state given to man to prove himself. But the crowning heresy of this "terrible decree" is its denial of agency. Moral agency—the right to choose—is central to God's plans for His children. Simply put, the God and Father of us all does not, will not, and indeed, by His very nature, cannot control His children by force. As He does not compel men to sin, neither does He compel them to righteousness. "God will force no man to heaven" (*Hymns,* No. 240). Man has the freedom to act for himself, the responsibility to act wisely, and the accountability for his actions.

Samuel the Lamanite prophet captured that idea in these words: "And now remember, remember, my brethren, that whosoever perisheth, perisheth unto himself; and whosoever doeth iniquity, doeth it unto himself; for behold, ye are free; ye are permitted to act for yourselves; for behold, God hath given unto you a knowledge and he hath made you free. He hath given unto you that ye might know good from evil, and he hath given unto you that ye might choose life or death; and ye can do good and be restored unto that which is good, or have that which is good restored unto you; or ye can do evil, and have that which is evil restored unto you" (Helaman 14:30–31).

Denying the damnable doctrine of predestination in no way diminishes the foreknowledge of God. In His omniscient wisdom, our Father has complete knowledge and understanding of the mind, will, and actions of each of His children. He to whom the past, present, and future are as one, knows what each of His offspring will do in each and every situation. He reads the future, both of individuals and of nations, with perfect clarity and total understanding. But He does not arbitrarily determine the future. He does not act as a sort of master puppeteer who manipulates his hapless subjects by jerking on the strings that control them. He weeps at our mistakes and sorrows at our foolishness but will not intervene to control us by force.

What has all of this to do with Jesus' actions as the foreordained Messiah? First and foremost, Jesus, like His father, both operates and is bound by the principle of agency. His very nature would not permit Him to act otherwise. Jesus' atoning vicarious sacrifice was both inspired by love and completely voluntary. As the Only Begotten Son of the Father in the flesh (John 3:16), He had the power of immortality. Through His mother, a mortal woman "most beautiful and fair above all other virgins" (1 Nephi 11:15), He inherited the ability to die. He had the power to live or to die—the choice was His. Jesus, who knew this principle perfectly, put it as follows: "I am the good shepherd, and know my sheep, and am known of mine. As the Father knoweth me, even so know I the Father: and I lay down my life for the sheep. Therefore doth my Father love me, because I lay down my life, that I might take it again. No man taketh it from me, but I lay it down of myself. I have power to lay it down, and I have power to take it again. This commandment have I received of my Father" (John 10:14–15, 17–18).

THE COUNCIL IN HEAVEN

Jesus' appointment to serve as the foreordained, promised Messiah was made at a great council in the heavens, held before the foundations of this earth were laid, and attended by all of the Father's spirit children. The council was held to announce the means whereby God's grand design—"to bring to pass the immortality and eternal life of man" (Moses 1:39)—might be realized. Elohim, the Eternal Father, had a plan to do so. The Father's plan of salvation—for He it was who ordained and established it—was taught to all of God's children. Each of us—and we were all there—was free to believe or not, to obey or not, as we chose.

The plan encompassed the creation of an earth, whereon God's children were to have the privilege of gaining mortal bodies. Mortality was given to mankind as a gift—a probationary period where each would be tried, tested, and tempted. The valor of each individual and his or her willingness to keep the Father's commandments would be determined. The plan also provided for a Savior—one of Elohim's spirit sons who would be born into mortality and, through an infinite and eternal atonement (see Alma 34:10–14), bring immortality to all and eternal life to the faithful.

Then, said the Father, "Whom shall I send?" (Abraham 3:27). Into this dramatic setting stepped two individuals, both mighty and powerful sons of the Father. One of them spake: "Father, thy will be done, and the glory be thine forever" (Moses 4:2). The speaker was Jehovah, He who would one day manifest Himself in the flesh as Jesus. In effect He said, "Father, I completely give my will to Thee. I will do as Thou wouldst have me do and will, in full accordance with Thy plan, atone for the sins of Thy children. And all the glory will be Thine."

Then a second came forward: "Here am I, send me, I will be thy son, and I will redeem all mankind, that one soul shall not be lost, and surely I will do it; wherefore give me thine honor" (Moses 4:1). There he stood—Lucifer, the Son of the Morning—proud, arrogant, ambitious, determined to usurp the Father's power, to have His honor. "I will exalt my throne above the stars of God. . . . I will ascend above the heights of the clouds; I will be like the most High" (Isaiah 14:13–14). What a contrast, not just in style, but in substance! Both candidates were mighty and great. But where one was meek and humble, the other was arrogant and ambitious. Where one was loving and compassionate, the other epitomized cruelty and force. One espoused agency, the other compulsion.

The Father spake, settling the matter by divine decree. "I will send the first" (Abraham 3:27). His beloved Son, Jehovah, chosen from the beginning, would be the atoning, redeeming Christ, the Savior and Deliverer, the foreordained Messiah.

Apostle Orson F. Whitney has described the events of that almost incomprehensibly grand council—the event from which all subsequent human experience flows, in these beautiful words:

> In solemn council sat the Gods; . . .
>
> Silence self-spelled; the hour was one
>   When thought doth most avail;
> Of worlds unborn the destiny
>   Hung trembling in the scale.
> Silence o'er all, and there arose,
>   Those kings and priests among,
> A Power sublime, than whom appeared
>   None nobler 'mid the throng.
>
> A stature mingling strength with grace,
>   Of meek though Godlike mien,
> The love-revealing countenance
>   Lustrous as lightning sheen;
> Whiter his hair than ocean spray,

Or frost of alpine hill.
He spake;—attention grew more grave,
   The stillness e'en more still.

"Father!"—the voice like music fell,
   Clear as the murmuring flow
Of mountain streamlet trickling down
   From heights of virgin snow.
"Father," it said, "since one must die,
   Thy children to redeem,
Whilst earth, as yet unformed and void,
   With pulsing life shall teem;

"And thou, great Michael, foremost fall,
   That mortal man may be,
And chosen Saviour yet must send,
   Lo, here am I—send me!
I ask, I seek no recompense,
   Save that which then were mine;
Mine be the willing sacrifice,
   The endless glory, Thine!" . . .

Silence once more. Then sudden rose
   Aloft a towering form,
Proudly erect as lowering peak
   'Lumed by the gathering storm;
A presence bright and beautiful,
   With eye of flashing fire,
A lip whose haughty curl bespoke
   A sense of inward ire.

"Give me to go!" thus boldly cried,
  With scarce concealed disdain;
"And hence shall none, from heaven to earth,
  That shall not rise again.
My saving plan exception scorns;
  Man's agency unknown;
As recompense, I claim the right
  To sit on yonder throne!"

Ceased Lucifer. The breathless hush
  Resumed and denser grew.
All eyes were turned; the general gaze
  One common magnet drew.
A moment there was solemn pause;
  Then, like the thunder-burst,
Rolled forth from lips omnipotent—
  From Him both last and first:

"Immanuel! thou my Messenger,
  Till time's probation end.
And one shall go thy face before,
  While twelve thy steps attend.
And many more, on that far shore,
  The pathway shall prepare,
That I, the First, the last may come,
  And earth my glory share." . . .

'T was done. From congregation vast
  Tumultuous murmurs rose;
Waves of conflicting sound, as when
  Two meeting seas oppose.

'T was finished. But the heavens wept;
   And still their annals tell
How one was choice of Elohim,
   O'er one who fighting fell.

("ELECT OF ELOHIM," IN *ELIAS: AN EPIC OF
THE AGES,* 30–34.)

Before we leave the great premortal council, it is necessary to emphasize two things. First, it must be understood that the *Father* is the author of the plan of salvation. It is His: He ordained it. He did not choose between two competing plans, one produced by Jesus and the other by Lucifer, the Prince of Darkness. It is consistent with what we know of the Father's omniscience to believe that He knew full well, beforehand, that Lucifer would seek to redeem God's children through compulsion. Most abhorrent of all, Satan would, if permitted, overthrow his Father and ascend to the throne of the Almighty. We can be certain this foreknowledge tore at the Father's heart. Yet, even though He knew that His son Lucifer's overweening arrogance would destroy him spiritually, the Father so honored the principle of agency that He did not intervene, though clearly He could have done so.

Sadly, Lucifer led the spirits that followed him—and they were one-third of the hosts of heaven—in open rebellion against the Father, the beloved Messiah-to-be, and the faithful spirit children who "[kept] their first estate" (Abraham 3:26). Of that rebellion, John the beloved apostle wrote: "And there was war in heaven: Michael and his angels fought against the dragon; and the dragon fought and his angels, and prevailed not; neither was their place found any more in heaven. And the great dragon was cast out, that old serpent, called the Devil, and Satan, which deceiveth the whole world: he was cast out into the earth, and his angels were cast out with him" (Revelation 12:7–9).

Secondly, the scriptures attest that it was Jehovah, He who would be born into the world as Jesus, who under the Father's direction created worlds without number (see Moses 1:31–33). "All things were made by him [that is, by Jesus, the Word of God]; and without him was not any thing made that was made" (John 1:3). Paul wrote to the

Hebrews: "The worlds were framed by the word of God" (Hebrews 11:3). Jesus, as the "Word of God" (see John 1:1) is, in effect, the executive through whom the word of the Father is put into effect in the creation of worlds.

The magnitude of those creations is simply beyond human comprehension. Astronomers tell us that the known universe is approximately 16 billion light years across and contains perhaps 100 billion galaxies. It is estimated that, on average, there are 100 billion stars in each galaxy. The galaxy of which our earth is part, the Milky Way, is thought to be comprised of perhaps 400 billion stars, with an estimated 300 billion planets that could support some form of life (see Carl Sagan, *Cosmos*, 298–301). Truly, God's works are "innumerable . . . unto man" (Moses 1:35). I find it impossible to dispute the idea that there is intelligent life "out there" among the stars, and beyond. We know nothing about the locations or the inhabitants of other worlds, except that those who dwell thereon are "begotten sons and daughters unto God" (D&C 76:24). The atoning sacrifice of Jesus, *wrought on this earth,* permits the inhabitants of "worlds without number" to be adopted into the family of God, spiritually begotten of Christ (Moses 5:7).

THE PROPHETS FORETOLD THE PROMISED MESSIAH WOULD COME

The earthly advent of the foreordained Messiah had long been predicted by God's prophets. To Adam, the great patriarch of our race, an angel of the Lord revealed that the Only Begotten Son of the Father would come to earth: "And after many days an angel of the Lord appeared unto Adam, saying: Why dost thou offer sacrifices unto the Lord? And Adam said unto him: I know not, save the Lord commanded me. And then the angel spake, saying: This thing is a similitude of the sacrifice of the Only Begotten of the Father, which is full of grace and truth. Wherefore, thou shalt do all that thou doest in the name of the Son, and thou shalt repent and call upon God in the name of the Son forevermore" (Moses 5:6–8).

And so it went—from Adam to Enoch to Abraham, Jacob, and Moses; from Moses to Isaiah and Jeremiah; down to John the Baptist, whose ministry immediately preceded that of Christ. All of the Hebrew prophets testified of the coming of the Great Messiah. They told of His atonement and declared Him to be the Son of God and Redeemer of the world. The sacrifice of the paschal lamb at the Jewish Passover was symbolic of the Lamb of God, who in due time would be slain for the sins of all. Christ's sacrifice, through the shedding of His blood in Gethsemane and on the cross, led Paul the Apostle to affirm in poetic majesty "for even Christ our passover is sacrificed for us" (1 Corinthians 5:7).

Space does not permit an exhaustive review of the Old Testament predictions of the coming of Jesus "to dwell upon His footstool among the sons of men." But the words of Isaiah, so rich in poetic imagery, so poignant in their expression, deserve special mention: Looking down through the mists of time to the great day of Christ's advent, the prophet exulted: "For unto us a child is born, unto us a son is given: and the government shall be upon his shoulder: and his name shall be called Wonderful, Counsellor, The mighty God, The everlasting Father,

The Prince of Peace" (Isaiah 9:6). But Isaiah saw more than a wondrous child: He saw one who "is despised and rejected of men; a man of sorrows, and acquainted with grief: and we hid as it were our faces from him; he was despised, and we esteemed him not. Surely he hath borne our griefs, and carried our sorrows. . . . He was wounded for our transgressions, he was bruised for our iniquities: the chastisement of our peace was upon him; and with his stripes we are healed" (Isaiah 53:3–5).

Prophets in ancient America also foretold the birth of the promised foreordained Messiah. Their predictions of His birth are capped by the miraculous visit of the resurrected Christ to the Americas. But more of that later.

The great Nephi recorded a revelation received by his father, Lehi: "Yea, even six hundred years from the time that my father left Jerusalem, a prophet would the Lord God raise up among the Jews—even a Messiah, or, in other words, a Savior of the world" (1 Nephi 10:4). Nephi wrote later, not as his father's scribe but in his own role as prophet, seer, and revelator, of a great vision he was permitted to view.

Nephi saw the circumstances of the Savior's birth; His ministry among men; His miraculous healings; His death on the cross; and the opposition faced by His faithful apostles, who would battle against the wickedness of the world (see 1 Nephi 11). Other Nephite prophets—including Jacob, the brother of Nephi; Abinadi; Benjamin; the great Alma; and Samuel, the Lamanite prophet—each in his turn proclaimed the coming of the Lamb of God.

Five years before the birth of the Babe in faraway Judea, Samuel the Lamanite said: "Behold, I give unto you a sign; for five years more cometh, and behold, then cometh the Son of God to redeem all those who shall believe on his name. And behold, this will I give unto you for a sign at the time of his coming; for behold, there shall be great lights in heaven, insomuch that in the night before he cometh there shall be no darkness, insomuch that it shall appear unto man as if it was day. Therefore, there shall be one day and a night and a day, as if it were one day and there were no night; and this shall be unto you for a sign; . . . and it shall be the night before he is born. And behold, there shall a new star arise" (Helaman 14:2–5).

That He came, first as the Babe of Bethlehem and then, after His mortal ministry was completed, to others as the risen, redeeming Christ of the empty sepulchre, provides positive proof of Jesus' divinity.

On both hemispheres ancient prophets proclaimed one central truth: through Jesus and Him alone is salvation provided, death conquered, and man made free. As the Apostle Peter pronounced: "Neither is there salvation in any other: for there is none other name under heaven given among men, whereby we must be saved" (Acts 4:12; see also Mosiah 3:17).

Those interested in a more complete review of the scriptural prophecies concerning the advent of the promised Messiah are referred to the article by D. Kelly Ogden and R. Val Johnson ("All the Prophets Prophesied of Christ," *Ensign*, Jan. 1994, 31–37), which lists many, but not all, scriptural passages that foretold the Messiah's advent many years, even centuries, before He came.

EVENTS SURROUNDING THE BIRTH OF JESUS

In addition to ancient prophecies that the Messiah would come, the scriptures contain an account of the sacred events associated with His birth, events that were full of portent for those who had ears to hear and eyes to see. We read that there was, in the days of Herod, the King of Judea, a certain priest named Zacharias, a priest of the Aaronic order. He and his wife, Elisabeth, were childless and beyond normal childbearing years. One day, as Zacharias carried out his priestly duties in the temple, there appeared to him a heavenly being, who proclaimed himself to be the angel Gabriel. Gabriel assured the old man that his prayers and those of his wife for a child had been heard. Elisabeth would yet bear a son and would call him John. He would be no ordinary mortal, for he would be a blessing to the people, mighty in the sight of God, filled with the Holy Ghost, and commissioned by God to prepare the way for the coming of the Messiah. Of the life of that great man we have only the barest of records, but we know him as John the Baptist, who cried repentance to the people and testified of Jesus: "He that cometh after me is mightier than I, whose shoes I am not worthy to bear: he shall baptize you with the Holy Ghost, and with fire" (Matthew 3:11).

Six months after the visitation of Gabriel to Zacharias, while Elisabeth was pregnant with her promised son, Gabriel was sent again to earth, on an even more glorious mission. He came to a young woman named Mary, a teenager who lived in Nazareth, a town in Galilee. She was of the lineage of the great King David. Although still an unmarried virgin, she was betrothed to a man named Joseph, himself of the royal Davidic lineage. To Mary the angel proclaimed: "Hail, thou that art highly favoured, . . . blessed art thou among women. . . . Fear not, Mary: for thou hast found favour with God. And behold, thou shalt . . . bring forth a son, and shalt call his name Jesus. And he shall reign over the house of Jacob for ever; and of his kingdom there shall be no end" (Luke 1:28, 30–31, 33).

Who can imagine the thoughts that must have flooded Mary's heart and mind as she listened to the angel? In the Jewish community in which she lived, the law regarded an unmarried woman who became pregnant as an adulteress, subject to death by stoning. It is certain that Mary did not yet fully comprehend the full meaning of the angel's message. Completely aside from that, Mary knew she was innocent of any sexual sin, but who would believe her story? Would Joseph, to whom she was betrothed, believe her, or would he make a public example of her out of a sense of betrayal? It speaks well of Joseph that, rather than make of Mary a public spectacle, he desired to release or divorce her secretly. Obviously he loved her deeply. But an angel of the Lord appeared to him in a dream and assured him that Mary's unborn son was not conceived in sin, but "is of the Holy Ghost" (Matthew 1:20), the Only Begotten of the Father in the flesh. Joseph, a just and good man, married Mary. In due time, as the scriptures recount, Mary did bring forth a son. And that single birth would change the world forever.

Sometime after the birth of Jesus, Herod, the cruel tyrant who was king of Judea, heard reports that a child had been born who was destined to become King of the Jews. Given the natural paranoia of tyrants, Herod, not surprisingly, considered this report, if true, to represent a threat to his blood-stained throne. He sent for wise men who had come from the east to Jerusalem, on a sacred search: "Where is he that is born King of the Jews? For we have seen his star in the east, and are come to worship him" (Matthew 2:2). Where is the baby? Herod wanted to know, and was told Bethlehem was the purported birthplace of the holy child. Go and find him, the tyrant directed—and let me know, so "I may come and worship him also" (Matthew 2:8). Herod, of course, had no intention of worshipping the baby. He wanted to murder him, as he had so many others whom he deemed to be a threat to his power, including his brother-in-law, wife, and several sons.

The wise men, following the new star, which pointed the way, came to Mary and her child and fell down and worshipped Him. Then, "being warned of God in a dream that they should not return to Herod, they departed into their own country another way" (Matthew 2:12).

Who were they, these wise men out of the East?

Neither scripture nor recorded history gives us their names or number. But tradition says there were three of them, named Balthasar, Melchior, and Gaspar (or Casper). Tradition avers also that they were kings, Balthasar of Arabia, Melchior of Persia, and Gaspar of India. On the other hand, Elder Bruce R. McConkie suggests they may have been "true prophets, righteous persons . . . to whom Deity revealed that the promised Messiah had been born among men" (*Doctrinal New Testament Commentary,* 1:103). If they were indeed kings, prophets, or even wise men, familiar with the ways of the world, they would no doubt have been wary and perhaps even a little afraid of Herod, whose bloody reputation must have been well-known. They were, after all, far from home, strangers in a strange land. They and their retinue of servants and bodyguards must have kept a watchful eye and looked well to their weapons until they were safely away from Herod and his henchmen.

Joseph, also warned of Herod's evil designs, fled in turn, with his wife and child, to Egypt. True to his vicious nature, Herod ordered the death of all children two years of age or less who dwelled in Bethlehem or surrounding regions. Although this slaughter of the innocents is not recorded in secular history, there is no doubt Herod was capable of such a frightful atrocity. Five days before his death, he ordered the arrest of many innocent citizens and gave orders they should be executed the day he died. In his demented mind, this would guarantee proper mourning in the country. Killing helpless infants in Bethlehem would not disconcert Herod!

The story of Jesus' birth recorded in Luke's gospel tells of an old man, Simeon, to whom it had been revealed that he would not see death until he had seen the Christ. When, in keeping with the Jewish custom, Jesus was brought by Mary and Joseph to the temple to be circumcised, Simeon, who had come "by the Spirit into the temple," recognized in the Baby Jesus the long-promised Messiah. Raising the child reverently in his arms, the old man exclaimed, "Lord, now lettest thou thy servant depart in peace, . . . for mine eyes have seen thy salvation, . . . a light to lighten the Gentiles, and the glory of thy people Israel" (Luke 2:29–32). Through the spirit of prophecy, Simeon was given to know that a new force had come into the world. Here, in this baby, lay the future. Simeon had thus seen God's salvation. Though Jesus would be rejected and scorned by most of His contemporaries, in the glory of His humility He condescended to live among the children of men. Teacher, exemplar, miracle worker, man of sorrows, He became the Atoning Savior of the world and the Resurrected Living Lord. All who "come and see"—be they shepherds, sinners, wise men, or prophets—will find Him, but only if they seek Him with real intent. In the next several chapters, we will consider some aspects of His life and death.

CHAPTER TWO

COME AND SEE . . . THE CARING, COMPASSIONATE SHEPHERD

The Lord my pasture will prepare,
And feed me with a shepherd's care.
His presence will my wants supply,
And guard me with a watchful eye.
My noon-day walks he will attend,
And all my silent midnight hours defend.
HYMNS, NO. 109

Of all the attempts by the writers of Holy Writ to capture in a single phrase the character and personality of Jesus, perhaps the most expressive is a term He used to describe Himself: "I am the good shepherd," He said, "[I] know my sheep, and am known of mine" (John 10:14). Jesus' description of Himself as the good shepherd would not have sounded strange to His listeners. Sheep and shepherds were no enigma to the pastoral peoples of ancient times.

Every Israelite, city-dwellers and farm folk alike, lived close to the rhythms of the flock and field, to the unending cycle of the seasons, the ebb and flow of good years and bad, the inevitable progression of plant and animal life from birth to death. Each had been taught from childhood the grand old stories of the great patriarchs of Hebrew history—heroes such as Abraham, Isaac, and Jacob—who were themselves men of the shepherd's crook and staff. Every Israelite had sung the praises of David, the comely shepherd boy who had slain the Philistine giant, Goliath, and became one of Israel's greatest kings (see 1 Samuel 17). The beloved words of the psalmist "The Lord is my shepherd; I shall not want" (Psalm 23:1) were familiar to one and all.

Each day, under the watchful eyes of family, friends, and neighbors, faithful shepherds led their flocks out to pasture, perhaps carrying one or more of the smaller and weaker lambs in their arms. During the day, as the sheep grazed on the hillsides or in the meadows, the shepherd dared not doze under a tree. He had to be ever on the alert for attempts by predators—the bear, the wolf, the lion, and the eagle—to ravage his little flock. Under his watchful eye, thieves dared not attempt to steal one or more of the sheep. Observers of those bucolic scenes had the quiet assurance that at dusk, without fail, each shepherd would lead his flock homeward, to the safety and security of the sheepfold. Such scenes were all part of the unvarying rhythms and deeply satisfying certainties of a pastoral life.

Jesus taught the difference between the hireling, with no sense of obligation or commitment to those in his charge, and the faithful shepherd, who was prepared, if need be, to lay down his life in protecting and defending his sheep. His listeners must have understood—at one level at least—the intent of the Savior's teaching. Perhaps some of them smiled, in fond remembrance of the days when they themselves had cared for sheep. Perhaps they recalled with wry humor how exasperating sheep can be, how stubbornly and foolishly they can behave, how much they act, in contradiction to all that's reasonable, just like sheep! Few there were, however, who saw beyond Jesus' homely figure of speech and superb teaching technique to the deeper reality that He, the compassionate, caring shepherd, would culminate His earthly ministry by sacrificing His sinless life. Few of them saw Him in His true character as the "Shepherd and Bishop of [our] souls," in the Apostle Peter's felicitous phrase (1 Peter 2:25).

Jesus' ministry, from first to last, was one filled with caring and compassion. All that He did was done out of love: "For he loveth the world, even that he layeth down his own life that he may draw all men unto him" (2 Nephi 26:24). As He went about healing and blessing all, Jesus demonstrated the power of God, to be sure, but His miracles stand also as symbols of His compassion for the weak, the unfortunate, those in spiritual or physical pain. His heart was ever tender and full of empathy for those in distress. The tears of the bereaved, the widow, and the orphan affected Him deeply. The depth of His love for children can never be plumbed. He, whose burdens were beyond our mortal abilities to comprehend, reached out in loving compassion to ease the cares of others, taking no thought of Himself. "Come unto me, all ye that labour and are heavy laden," He said, "and I will give you rest. Take my yoke upon you, and learn of me; for I am meek and lowly in heart: and ye shall find rest unto your souls. For my yoke is easy, and my burden is light" (Matthew 11:28–30).

How can we ever thank Him enough for the example and gift of His life? Objectively, of course, we cannot. King Benjamin spoke to this point in his great valedictory sermon: "I say unto you that if ye should serve him who has created you from the beginning, and is preserving you from day to day, by lending you breath, that ye may live and move and do according to your own will, and even supporting you from one moment to another—I say, if ye should serve him with all your whole souls yet ye would be unprofitable servants" (Mosiah 2:21).

Note well: "unprofitable servants," despite all we can do! One of the best expressions of our devotion is to give away all our sins to know Him (see Alma 22:18), surrendering our will to His, forsaking all, that we might be counted as one of His disciples (see Luke 14:33).

He calls upon us to wear out our lives in trying to serve Him and His cause. What is that cause? The

Lord's own statement comes to mind: "This is my work and my glory—to bring to pass the immortality and eternal life of man: (Moses 1:39). President J. Reuben Clark Jr. further explained: "[The Savior] left as a heritage to those . . . in his Church the carrying on of . . . two great things—work for the relief of the ills and the sufferings of humanity, and the teaching of the spiritual truths which should bring us back into the presence of our Heavenly Father" (in CR, Apr. 1937, 22).

The world is filled with so many problems, so much injustice, so much sorrow, so many tears. It would be so easy to say, "Lord, it's hopeless. I just can't do it. I don't have the strength. There's just too much to do." To such, Jesus' counsel is clear: Every journey starts with a single step. Try as he or she will, no individual can do all that needs to be done to dry every tear and right every wrong. Jesus doesn't expect that of us. But His charge is clear: we are to love those less fortunate than ourselves, one at a time. And others can do their part in turn. We are to be diligent, seek ways to help, and use our own initiative. In His own words: "It is not meet that I should command in all things; for he that is compelled in all things, the same is a slothful and not a wise servant; wherefore he receiveth no reward. Verily I say, men should be anxiously engaged in a good cause, and do many things of their own free will, and bring to pass much righteousness; for the power is in them" (D&C 58:26–28).

John the beloved apostle recorded that "there are also many other things which Jesus did, the which, if they should be written every one, I suppose that even the world itself could not contain the books that should be written" (John 21:25).

Such is Jesus' compassion as the caring shepherd. No words of tongue or pen can do His goodness justice. Yet there are, perhaps, five of His acts of mercy that illustrate, in a generic sort of way, His role as the compassionate, all-merciful shepherd.

The first concerns His dealing with the woman taken in adultery; the second the healing of the paralytic at the pool of Bethesda; the third the raising of Lazarus from the dead; and the fourth His loving compassion for the Nephite children. The last example deals with the lost sheep and the compassionate shepherd who sought for it in the wilderness. Let us consider each example.

1. THE WOMAN TAKEN IN ADULTERY
(JOHN 8:1–12)

It was the autumn of the year, and the Feast of Tabernacles was near at hand. This ancient feast was the third of the great festivals that marked the Jewish year, the others being the Passover and Pentecost. At each of the three feasts, every Israelite male was expected to appear before the Lord in formal celebration. The Feast of Tabernacles was both a memorial of the long days of wandering in the wilderness and a celebration of the current harvest. Seven days, each marked by special services of thanksgiving and praise, were followed by an eighth day, which featured a solemn procession of priests who circled the altar of the temple seven times.

Jesus went to the feast, traveling "not openly but as it were in secret" (John 7:10). There was much speculation among those in the crowd attending the sacred event about whether Jesus was the Messiah, a prophet, or just another in the long line of deceivers who had long plagued the Jewish nation. After the festivities associated with the feast were over, Jesus went to the temple one morning early. As

He sat there, probably in the Court of the Women, a colonnaded enclosure within the inner courts open to Israelites of both sexes, people crowded around Him, anxious to hear His preaching. His teaching was interrupted by the arrival of a party of scribes and Pharisees, bringing with them a woman.

They sat her in the midst of the group and proclaimed she had been taken in adultery, "in the very act" (John 8:4). What should be done with her, they asked, noting that Moses had commanded adulterers were to be stoned.

Clearly, the scribes and Pharisees were not really interested in Jesus' counsel on the matter. The whole affair was a put-up job, an attempt to ensnare Jesus. If He agreed the woman should be stoned (and assuredly her partner as well, since the Mosaic Law required equal punishment for both), He would be accused of attempting to usurp the exclusive right of the Roman overlords to inflict the death penalty. Jesus' opponents would have liked nothing better than to portray Him as one in opposition to the existing civil authority. On the other hand, if He counseled she should not be stoned, He would be charged with disrespecting the great Moses. *We have him now,* they must have thought. But of course Jesus was not to be caught in such a transparent scheme.

At first He paid no attention to the accusers, tracing on the ground with His finger. Then, in response to their repeated questioning, He rose and said simply, "He that is without sin among you, let him first cast a stone at her" (John 8:7). Jesus knew full well that under Mosaic Law (Deuteronomy 17:6–7), it was the duty of the witness-accusers to begin the work of execution by casting the first stone. He knew also the sin-laden lives of the woman's accusers, who were guilty, either actually or in their hearts, of the very sin charged against her.

The accusers, who had been so intent on using the unfortunate woman as a pawn in their diabolical scheme, drew back in shame, "convicted by their own conscience" (John 8:9). Cowards all, they slunk away, humiliated and exposed publicly for the sinful hypocrites they were. Jesus was left alone, save for the woman.

"Where are those thine accusers?" He asked. "Hath no man condemned thee?"

"No man, Lord," she replied, I'm sure both in relief and wonderment.

"Neither do I condemn thee," said Jesus. "Go; and sin no more" (John 8:10–11).

This incident is often used by those who attempt to gloss over the consequences of sin, to say in effect, "Don't worry about it; God is generous and will forgive, as Jesus forgave the adulterous woman." But it is important to note that Jesus neither condoned the woman's sin, nor forgave her of it. From the depths of His mercy and compassion, He simply adjured her to change her ways—to sin no more.

Was she repentant? Perhaps in part, but full repentance, while certainly attainable for the sin she had committed, requires recognition, remorse, restitution, and firm resolve not to commit that sin again. All of these take time to demonstrate and intense, prolonged effort to accomplish. It is simply not possible, from John's record, to determine the depth of the woman's repentance. Her salutation of Jesus as "Lord" suggests, however, that she recognized Him as the Anointed One with the power to forgive sins. We can be certain she was grateful for His intervention, which spared her an especially gruesome death. We can only hope that she did indeed repent fully and change her life. In this regard it is heartening to note that in Joseph Smith's inspired translation of John 8:11, the Prophet added this sentence: "And the woman glorified God from that hour, and believed on his name."

As Jesus was slow to condemn, so too must we be righteous in our judgments of others. One of the ironies of life is that many want forgiveness for their own sins, while expecting others to meet a more strict standard, to carry forever the weight of their sins. Elder Boyd K. Packer reflected on this matter at the April 1979 general conference of the Church:

"At times someone has come to me, their faith shaken by alleged wrongdoing of some leader in the Church.

"For instance, one young man was being constantly ridiculed by his co-workers for his activity in the Church. They claimed to know of a bishop who had cheated someone in business, or a stake president who had misrepresented something on a contract, or a mission president who had borrowed money, giving false information.

"Or, they told of a bishop who had discriminated against one member, refusing to give a temple recommend, but had shown favoritism by signing a recommend for another whose unworthiness was widely known. . . .

"When you hear stories, be wise. Unless you are in all the interviews, and hear all the evidence, you are not in a position to really know. Be careful, lest you jump to a confusion.

"Unless you are a participant and have full knowledge, better:

"'Judge not, that ye be not judged.

"'For with what judgment ye judge, ye shall be judged' (Matthew 7:1–2)" (in CR, Apr. 1979, 109–11).

2. THE HEALING OF THE PARALYTIC MAN
(JOHN 5:1–17)

During the second year of His mortal ministry, Jesus went from Galilee to Jerusalem, probably at the Feast of the Passover. The narrow, twisted streets of the city would have been packed with pilgrims, filled with a cacophony of noise, the air pungent with a thousand smells, some pleasant, others repugnant. He came, on a sabbath morning, to a pool called, in the Aramaic tongue, *Bethesda*, around which there were five porches. On the terraces leading to the water's edge lay a multitude of diseased, disfigured, and dying people. Each was there in the desperate hope that he or she could be healed.

The pool, probably a mineral spring, was reputed to possess curative powers. Periodically the surface of the water would become agitated, and then recede. Superstition had it that an angel of God "troubled the water" and that whoever first stepped into the pool after the disturbance of the water's surface would be healed. Each of the pitiful sufferers who lay or crouched at the water's edge focused all attention on the pool's surface, pinning all of his or her hopes on the chance of being first into the water once the agitation started. Each must have been totally preoccupied, intent only on that task. We can be sure that nobody paid attention to the man who suddenly appeared before them.

So it is with many of us. We are often so preoccupied with our own problems, so caught up with our own difficulties, so disabled by our sins or fears, that we fail to notice, in our midst, the presence of the caring, compassionate healer of our souls.

Among the crush of broken, diseased, and helpless bodies around the pool, there lay a man who had been infirm for thirty-eight years. It seems he was paralyzed, perhaps from polio or some other debilitating disorder. Whatever the cause of his affliction, the man had dragged his weakened, emaciated body to the pool's edge every day for years. So crippled was he, that lacking a friend or servant to help him into the water, his hope of being first was repeatedly dashed. Someone else always beat him, and his dream of being healed must have shrunk each day. Yet, somehow, hoping where there was no hope, he persisted in his vain search for healing. On this man Jesus fastened His gaze.

Why, out of all those present that Sabbath day, did Jesus notice this particular pitiful man? In that place of total and overwhelming misery and sorrow, why did Jesus single out one sufferer above another? Perhaps it was the despair, the hopelessness, the desperate longing in the man's eyes that attracted

Jesus' attention. Perhaps it was the overwhelming need, the abject helplessness, that caught the Savior's eye. The man had done all he could to help himself but without success. Only the "Help of the helpless" could provide the needed succor. Perhaps those are the same reasons Jesus notices you and me. He sees our needs. He feels our pain. He recognizes when we can go no further on our own strength and stands ready to lift and empower us. He longs for us to notice Him and bring Him into our lives.

"Behold, I stand at the door, and knock: if any man hear my voice, and open the door, I will come in to him, and will sup with him, and he with me" (Revelation 3:20).

Jesus spoke: "Wilt thou be made whole?" (John 5:6).

Notice Jesus did not say, "Do you need to be made whole?" Of course the man, crippled as he was, needed to be healed if he were ever to walk! But Jesus' words were purposeful: they focused the man's full attention on the Master, arousing in him that spark of faith, which however dim it had become

42

after years of hopeless despair, now burst forth again into full flame.

Sensing the man's faith, Jesus commanded: "Rise, take up thy bed, and walk.

"And immediately the man was made whole, and took up his bed, and walked: and on the same day was the sabbath" (John 5:8–9).

I have no doubt that the man, after a few tentative, almost disbelieving steps, jumped and danced and ran in the joy of his newfound strength, praising God for the blessings that had come to him.

The Pharisees who saw the man in his recovered state, doubtless striding along with his bed on his shoulders, groused and complained. It was, they charged, against Mosaic Law "to carry thy bed" on the sabbath.

How dare Jesus heal a man on the sabbath? Blind hypocrites all, they failed to understand that the sabbath was made for man and not man for the sabbath.

The healing of the paralyzed man at the pool provides powerful witness of Jesus' ability to bring healing to the helpless and hopeless. But the bestowal of that blessing is dependent on our faith, our willingness to open the door and let Jesus into our lives. Furthermore, though the bestowal of the blessing of healing was instantaneous for the paralyzed man, God works His miracles in His time, not ours. Not all righteously sought-after blessings are attained in this life, but the prayers of the righteous are *always* heard, and *always* answered, in *His* time, and in His way.

3. THE RAISING OF LAZARUS FROM THE DEAD
(JOHN 11:1–46)

Jesus' raising of Lazarus from the dead is one of the great miracles of His ministry, though it is actually the third recorded instance of His restoring a dead person to life.

The story is well-known. There was a certain family, Lazarus and his two sisters, Mary and Martha, who lived in the village of Bethany, a few miles distance from Jerusalem. Jesus customarily stayed at their home when in the village. He seems to have had a very close, loving relationship with Lazarus and his two sisters. They were dear to Him and He to them.

Then tragedy struck. Lazarus fell ill. His two distraught sisters sent a message to their beloved friend: "Lord, behold, he whom thou lovest is sick" (v. 3). It seems that by the time Jesus received this message, Lazarus had already died.

On hearing of His friend's misfortune, Jesus remarked: "This sickness is not unto death, but for the glory of God, that the Son of God might be glorified thereby" (v. 4).

It is apparent Jesus already knew that Lazarus had died and was determined to restore him to life. The miracle—for such it had to be—would be irrevocable proof, for all to see, of Jesus' sovereignty over death.

After two days, Jesus said to the disciples, "Let us go into Judaea again. . . . Lazarus is dead. . . . nevertheless let us go unto him" (vv. 7, 14–15). (Jesus and His followers were then in Perea, east of the Jordan River.)

Upon the Master's approach, one of the grieving sisters, Martha, ran to meet Jesus and His followers.

"Lord," she said, "if thou hadst been here, my brother had not died" (v. 21).

Jesus reassured her: "Thy brother shall rise again" (v. 23).

Martha, thinking Jesus was speaking only in soothing generalities, replied, "I know he shall rise again in the resurrection at the last day."

Then spake Jesus, Lord over life and death, these solemn words of grace and power: "I am the resurrection, and the life: he that believeth in me, though he were dead, yet shall he live: and whosoever liveth and believeth in me shall never die" (vv. 24–25).

This simple yet profound statement lies at the very core of the Christian gospel. It brings hope to every soul who harkens to it. It encapsulates not only the sure and certain hope that the enemy of death is conquered through Christ's atonement, but provides vivid testimony of Jesus' messianic role.

Mary, the other sister, also overcome with grief, ran to meet Jesus, expressing a similar emotion to that of Martha: "Lord, if thou hadst been here, my brother had not died" (v. 32).

The tears of these two righteous women moved the Savior to sorrow, and He too wept. Some of the unbelieving onlookers queried, in their malevolent, carping way, why Jesus, who had opened the eyes of the blind, could not have saved the life of Lazarus.

Jesus demonstrated His unparalleled power in a way even the most cynical observer could not doubt. Calling upon those present to take away the stone that covered the opening to the tomb wherein Lazarus lay, Jesus cried out in a loud voice, "Lazarus, come forth" (v. 43).

Miracle of miracles, the dead man, now restored to life, came forth, bound hand and foot with burial clothes.

"Loose him, and let him go," (v. 44), Jesus commanded, and it was done.

Why did Jesus raise Lazarus from the dead? To be sure, He loved the man, and his two sisters, but the miracle of restoring life was not accomplished just to assuage the grief of the mourners. There was a higher purpose: to show the power of God and to testify to the messiahship of Jesus. As with most of His miracles, some observers believed, but others, darkened in mind and spirit, refused to be swayed in their malignant opposition to Jesus and His divine mission.

4. JESUS CARES FOR THE NEPHITE CHILDREN
(3 NEPHI 17:11)

After His death and resurrection Jesus visited the faithful Nephite remnant on the American continent. He declared to them His office as the Atoning Savior, the Light and Life of the world, who had glorified the Father in taking upon Himself the sins of the world (see 3 Nephi 11:11); called and commissioned twelve disciples with authority to teach and baptize; preached wondrous truths to those assembled; announced that the Nephites were the other sheep of whom He spake in Jerusalem (3 Nephi 15:21); and directed the people to ponder His words and pray for understanding. He healed the sick and afflicted, the lame, the blind, and the dumb. And then He revealed His special love for the little children.

He commanded the children to be brought forth and set them down upon the ground round about Him. The people, numbering about 2500 men, women, and children, knelt before Him, and Jesus prayed to the Father for them, using language so celestial that it "cannot be written" (3 Nephi 17:5).

After they arose from the earth, Jesus said: "Blessed are ye because of your faith. And now behold, my joy is full" (v. 20). Then He took the little children, one by one, and blessed them, and prayed unto the Father for them. And when He had done this "he wept, . . . and he spake unto the multitude, and said unto them: Behold your little ones. And as they looked to behold they cast their eyes towards heaven, and they saw the heavens open, and they saw angels descending out of heaven as it were in the midst of fire; and they came down and encircled those little ones about, and they were encircled about with fire; and the angels did minister unto them. And the multitude did see and hear and bear record" (3 Nephi 17:21, 23–25).

Why does Jesus so love little children? Perhaps it is because of their innocence, their lack of guile, their meek, humble, teachable natures (see Mosiah 3:19). Jesus understands fully that little children "cannot sin, for power is not given unto Satan to tempt little children, until they begin to become accountable before me; for it is given unto them even as I will" (D&C 29:47–48).

Speaking of children who die in their infancy, the prophet Joseph Smith stated views fully consistent with those of the Savior. Such children, the Prophet said, "were too pure, too lovely, to live on earth" (*Teachings of the Prophet Joseph Smith,* 196–97). Is it any wonder Jesus loves children?

Jesus knew of a certainty that children have a right to peace and security. The great prophet Isaiah intoned, "And all thy children shall be taught of the Lord; and great shall be the peace of thy children" (Isaiah 54:13). And Jesus Himself declared, "Even so it is not the will of your Father which is in heaven, that one of these little ones should perish" (Matthew 18:14).

Modern-day prophets echo the words and sentiments of Jesus in pleading on behalf of children. President Gordon B. Hinckley said: "My plea—and I wish I were more eloquent in voicing it—is a plea to save the children. Too many of them walk with pain and fear, in loneliness and despair. Children need sunlight. They need happiness. They need love and nurture. They need kindness and refreshment and affection. Every home, regardless of the cost of the house, can provide an environment of love which will be an environment of salvation" ("Save the Children," *Ensign*, Nov. 1994, 54).

5. THE NINETY AND NINE
(LUKE 15:4–7)

This story actually is one of three masterful parables recounted in Luke 15, the others being the parable of the lost coin, and perhaps Jesus' most well-known parable, that of the prodigal son. It was delivered during the third year of Jesus' ministry, during a time when He experienced both the adulation of the crowds and increasing opposition from the chief priests and other religious leaders.

In the parable, Jesus again refers to the now-familiar figure of the faithful shepherd. "What man of you, having an hundred sheep, if he lose one of them, doth not leave the ninety and nine in the wilderness, and go after that which is lost, until he find it? And when he hath found it, he layeth it on his shoulders, rejoicing. And when he cometh home, he calleth together his friends and neighbours, saying unto them, Rejoice with me; for I have found my sheep which was lost. I say unto you, that like-wise joy shall be in heaven over one sinner that repenteth, more than over ninety and nine just per-sons, which need no repentance" (Luke 15:4–7).

The story is sublime in its symbolism. Who could not be thrilled at the image of the courageous shep-herd, armed only with a curved staff for guiding the sheep, a rod used as a weapon, and a sling? (see Psalm 23:4; 1 Samuel 17:40). Leaving the relative security and safety of his home base, he ventures boldly out into the thickets and undergrowth of the wilderness to find the one that is lost. We can picture the faithful shepherd girding his cloak about himself as protection from the wind and the rain. Danger lurks out there in the darkness: those eyes that glow in the night, are they those of a lion or bear? No matter, the shepherd knows his duty, and off he goes, willing to take what-ever risk is involved to safeguard those in his charge.

But of course, at another, deeper level, the story is not about sheep at all. It is about lost souls and the Lord's servants who are given responsibility to care for them. Finding lost sheep and bringing them home safely (on the shepherd's shoulders, if needs be) is an intrinsic, eternal part of the shepherd's role. It is one of the most important tasks Christ assigns to faithful undershepherds.

Finding the sheep and bringing it safely back is, of course, a great miracle. But an even greater miracle is the ability of the Savior's love to heal spiritual wounds, to apply a balm of Gilead to sin-sick souls, to bring to full flower and fruition the shriveled bud of faith, which has perhaps long been smothered by the bitter weeds of worldly care.

SOME GENERAL PRINCIPLES FOR SHEPHERDS

Several principles undergird the tasks faced by faithful undershepherds, called to assist the caring, compassionate shepherd of our souls. They include the following:

THE WORTH OF SOULS IS GREAT IN THE SIGHT OF GOD

This well-known verse from D&C 18:10 is widely and wisely quoted in the context of missionary work. But the concept of the precious worth of souls applies also to the work of the shepherd as he labors with those already in the kingdom—those precious souls who already are numbered as lambs of the pasture and sheep of the fold of Christ. To Christ, *all* are important; He makes little distinction between those already in the Kingdom and those who have not yet entered. "He inviteth . . . all to come unto him and partake of his goodness" (2 Nephi 26:33). Jesus' loving concern for the Nephite children, for Lazarus His dead friend, or for the paralyzed man in the pool of Bethesda are but differing expressions of His unconditional and universal love. He loves us, warts and all. Nothing we can do will ever break the band of love that binds Him to us. As the Apostle Paul declared: "I am persuaded, that neither death, nor life, nor angels, nor principalities, nor powers, nor things present, nor things to come, nor height, nor depth, nor any other creature, shall be able to separate us from the love of God, which is in Christ Jesus our Lord" (Romans 8:38–39).

The shepherd, ever ready to go out into the wilderness in search of the one, knows well the importance of the ninety and nine who remain at home. He recognizes that most of them are "anxiously engaged," committed, striving each day to do their best. They are the faithful workaday members of the Church, who wear out their lives in humble, unheralded service to others and to God. Their faith is simple, yet profound. They are heroes and heroines, though they would blush if you called them such. Despite their faith and dedication, they need constant care and attention; Satan, who knows well "the weight of [their] calling," will try them. The shepherd, knowing that, is ever alert, ever vigilant. When he is required to leave the ninety and nine to seek after the lost, he is careful to ensure the flock is not left unattended, even for a minute. How foolish it would be, he knows, to retrieve the lost one and on returning home find the flock scattered and riven by vicious predators. The wise shepherd ensures that in his absence the sheep are properly cared for, by counselors, auxiliary leaders, home and visiting teachers, and other faithful undershepherds.

The second great principle undergirding the work of the shepherd is the following:

SERVICE TO OTHERS IS SERVICE TO GOD

Jesus' whole life was a testimony to the validity of this principle. His concern for the poor and needy, the widow and orphan, the blind, deaf and lame, the sorrowing mother or sister, capped by the incomprehensible service of His atoning sacrifice, together remind us that service is essential to salvation. Wise undershepherds, seeking to emulate the sublime example of the caring and compassionate Good Shepherd, find celestial joy in serving others. They learn that service drives out selfishness, the great enemy of spirituality. They understand that service allows us to reach into the deepest and finest attributes of our souls to become "partakers of the Divine nature."

Finally, wise shepherds understand the third great principle that guides their work. It is as follows:

PRACTICE "PATIENT CONTINUANCE IN WELL-DOING"

It takes time for people to change, for performance to improve, and for old habits and old ways to fall away. Wise shepherds are slow to judge and quick to forgive, as Jesus ever was. Perhaps that is why He did not condemn the woman taken in adultery, but counseled her to "go and sin no more." Wise shepherds know that enduring to the end means much more than dealing well with acute tribulation. It requires also a "patient continuance in well doing" (Romans 2:7). Over time those who strive with all their hearts to come unto Christ become as little children—"submissive, meek, humble, patient, full of love, willing to submit to all things" (Mosiah 3:19). Is it any wonder Jesus loved little children? As with all other virtues, the wellspring of patience is love. Jesus' love was perfect, all-encompassing. In this, as in all else that is virtuous, lovely, and of good report, He is the perfect exemplar.

Shepherds learn two other things: their timetables may not be those of God; and they never give up on people. They are particularly patient with those who struggle with tribulation, who suffer, patiently or otherwise. There are some whose afflictions are consecrated for their personal gain (see Nephi 2:2), but suffering in and of itself is not an effective teacher. These wise words of Anne Morrow Lindbergh merit mention: "I do not believe that sheer suffering teaches. If suffering alone taught, all the world would be wise, since everyone suffers. To suffering must be added mourning, understanding, patience, love, openness, and the willingness to remain vulnerable."

May all who are blessed to serve as Christ's undershepherds follow the ineffable example of love, patience, forgiveness, and the love of service exemplified in this sweet verse from a beloved hymn:

> Make us thy true undershepherds;
> Give us a love that is deep.
> Send us out into the desert,
> Seeking thy wandering sheep.
>
> *Hymns*, no. 221

Jesus, the caring, compassionate shepherd, sets for all time the standard for human behavior. He teaches us how to live and love and at the same time demonstrates both His own messianic calling and His Father's power and glory.

"Come and see"—and as you find Him, your own ability to serve as one of His faithful undershepherds will increase and your service to Him will be magnified. True happiness will be yours.

His actions and example as the Shepherd of Our Souls underline Jesus' role as the Living Water and the Bread of Life. We shall consider that aspect of His life and service in the next chapter.

CHAPTER THREE

COME AND SEE . . . THE LIVING WATER AND THE BREAD OF LIFE

While of this broken bread
Humbly we eat,
Our thoughts to thee are led
In rev'rence sweet.
Bruised, broken, torn for us
On Calvary's hill—
Thy suff'ring borne for us
Lives with us still.

As to our lips the cup
Gently we press,
Our hearts are lifted up,
Thy name we bless!
Guide us where'er we go,
Till in the end
Life ever-more we'll know
Through thee, our Friend.

HYMNS, NO. 181

Living in a parched land, Jesus used the symbolism of precious water in many of His teachings. He transformed water into wine at the wedding feast at Cana (John 2:7–9); spoke with Nicodemus about the need to be born of water and of the Spirit (John 3:5); told the Samaritan woman at Jacob's well that He (Jesus) was living water (John 4:10, 14); healed the man at the pool of Bethesda (John 5:3–7; see chapter two); and washed the disciples' feet (John 13:5).

Water, when used as a teaching tool, is a powerful image. After all, water is required for the support and survival of plant and animal life. Lack of it leads inevitably to death. Water, along with bread, has long been understood as the minimum nourishment necessary for human life. Furthermore, famine-producing droughts, caused by only slight variations in annual rainfall, were a frequent problem in Palestine throughout biblical times (see Genesis 26:1; 41:29–36; 1 Kings 17:1, 7). Jesus didn't have to explain to his listeners how precious water is.

JESUS SPEAKS TO NICODEMUS
(JOHN 3)

Jesus had gone from Capernaum to Jerusalem to attend the annual Passover celebration. Though it was still early in His ministry, many of the common people already believed in Him. Now, for the first time, one of the learned and great ones of Jewish society came surreptitiously to Jesus. His name was Nicodemus. He was a Pharisee, a member of the Sanhedrin. Evidently he was attracted to Jesus' teachings but lacked the courage to openly show his support. Probably, Nicodemus feared that he might lose his position of power and authority if he seemed to favor one whom the high priests viewed with disfavor. Accordingly, he came to Jesus by night, when he could slip in and out without being seen by others.

Nicodemus is an interesting character, not unlike many men of prominence in the world today. Though honest and sincere in his intentions, Nicodemus had at best a stunted faith. True, he later offered a not very energetic defense of Jesus (see John 7:50–53) and assisted Joseph of Arimathaea in preparing Jesus' body for burial (John 19:38–42; see chapter six); but his belief, based perhaps mostly on intellectualism, evidently never blossomed into true faith—the faith that goes beyond mere belief to resolution and which leads to action regardless of consequence or cost.

Nicodemus reminds me of a man President Hugh B. Brown met in England in September 1939. The Englishman was a very prominent member of society, a member of Parliament, a very well-respected lawyer, author of many learned texts on the law, and later a member of the British House of Lords. Without his family's knowledge, the man asked Brother Brown, then serving as president of the British Mission, to come to his office (not his home!) to talk about Salt Lake City and the Mormons. Brother Brown met with the man, and they had an animated and probing discussion about various aspects of the gospel. At the conclusion of their interview, the Englishman said, "Mr. Brown, I wonder if your people appreciate the import of your message. If what you have told me is true, it is the greatest message that has come to this earth since the angels announced the birth of Christ."

He then added: "I wish it were true. I hope it may be true. God knows it ought to be true. I would to God," he wept, "that some man could appear on earth and authoritatively say, 'Thus saith the Lord.'"

Their meeting ended. Brother Brown soon returned to America. Some time later the man became sufficiently interested in the gospel to request that Brother Brown baptize him when he returned to England. By the time Brother Brown returned to England, unfortunately the man had died, still unbaptized (*An Abundant Life: The Memories of Hugh B. Brown*, 92–95).

Nicodemus began the discussion by trying to flatter Jesus. "Rabbi, we know that thou art a teacher come from God: for no man can do these miracles that thou doest, except God be with him" (John 3:2). Jesus, who had little confidence in those whose belief was based on signs and wonders, rocked Nicodemus with His reply: "Verily, verily, I say unto thee, except a man be born again, he cannot see the kingdom of God" (John 3:3).

Born again! What could that mean? Nicodemus, who seemed genuinely puzzled by Jesus' comment asked, "How can a man be born when he is old? Can he enter the second time into his mother's womb, and be born?" (John 3:4).

Nicodemus' reply seems at first glance to be obtuse. He knew, of course, that Jesus' statement could not be taken literally. He knew also that every Gentile converted to Judaism was considered to be newborn. The symbol of a new birth thus was in common usage in Jewish society. Most probably, Nicodemus was concerned that Jesus spoke as though *every* person—Jew and Greek, bond and free, black and white—was to be treated alike. *All* had to be born again to see the kingdom of God. This idea flew in the face of long-established Jewish notions of religious exclusivity. Surely Jesus could not mean that no special privileges were given to Jews! After all, were they not the chosen people of God?

Jesus repeated His assertion: "Except a man be born of water and of the Spirit, he cannot enter into the kingdom of God. That which is born of the flesh is flesh; and that which is born of the Spirit is spirit. Marvel not that I said unto thee, ye must be born again" (John 3:5–7).

There could be no mistaking Jesus' meaning.

Everyone, with no exceptions arising from race, gender, ethnicity, or status, must be born again to enter the kingdom of God. (Incidentally, as President Joseph Fielding Smith points out, the "kingdom of God" Jesus refers to clearly is the celestial kingdom described in D&C 76 [see *Answers to Gospel Questions,* 5:147–48]. That entrance, that rebirth, comes about through the joint actions of water and of the Spirit. The water referred to is the water of baptism. "Being born again, comes by the Spirit of God through ordinances," the prophet Joseph Smith said (*History of the Church,* 3:392). Baptism is the golden door that leads to the celestial kingdom of God. Those who come in at the door, repentant and contrite, are made clean, their sins washed away by the atoning blood of Christ. They become new creatures.

Father Adam inquired of the Lord, "Why is it that men must repent and be baptized in water?" (Moses 6:53). In reply, he was told to teach this great truth to his children (and by extension to all of the children of men in every generation): "That by reason of transgression cometh the fall, which fall bringeth death, and inasmuch as ye were born into the world by water, and blood, and the spirit, which I have made, and so became of dust a living soul, even so ye must be born again into the kingdom of heaven, of water, and of the Spirit, and be cleansed by blood, even the blood of mine Only Begotten; that ye might be sanctified from all sin, and enjoy the words of eternal life in this world, and eternal life in the world to come, even immortal glory; For by the water ye keep the commandment; by the Spirit ye are justified, and by the blood ye are sanctified" (Moses 6:59–60).

As Adam learned, three elements—water, blood, and Spirit—are associated with birth into the kingdom of God. These three join together in perfect unity to testify of Christ's atoning sacrifice and act in similitude of it. The sacred ordinance of baptism is carried out by immersing the candidate in water. Insofar as blood is concerned, be it noted that Jesus sweat great drops of blood in the agony of Gethesmane. Additionally, when He died on the cross, a Roman soldier "pierced his side, and forthwith came there out blood and water" (John 19:34).

But what of the Spirit? Jesus voluntarily "gave up

the ghost" (John 19:30) on the cross, permitting temporary separation of body and spirit. Furthermore, those who enter baptism with a broken heart and contrite spirit have received testimony of the Spirit that Christ is indeed the redeeming, atoning Savior.

The new birth, which is made possible by baptism, is symbolic of a new life in the kingdom of God. The atonement of Christ makes it possible for those baptized to be reborn. Baptism is performed in similitude of the death, burial, and resurrection of Jesus. The Apostle Paul explained: "Know ye not, that so many of us as were baptized into Jesus Christ were baptized into his death? Therefore we are buried with him by baptism into death: that like as Christ was raised up from the dead by the glory of the Father, even so we also should walk in newness of life. For if we have been planted together in the likeness of his death, we shall be also *in the likeness* of his resurrection: knowing this, that our old man is crucified with him, that the body of sin might be destroyed, that henceforth we should not serve sin. . . . Now if we be dead with Christ, we believe that we shall also live with him" (Romans 6:3–8; emphasis added). Paul's references to burial clearly indicate the accepted mode of baptism. For the symbolism to be complete, baptism must be by immersion, if it is to be in similitude of the death, burial, and resurrection of Christ. This indeed is the only procedure authorized by Jesus Himself (see 3 Nephi 19:11–12; D&C 20:73–74). It surely goes without saying that more than good form and good intentions are required for a baptism to be considered effective in the eyes of God. The person conducting the sacred ordinance must be authorized to do so, by someone who himself is a legal administrator in God's kingdom.

Being born again certainly can happen almost instantaneously as occurred, for example, with Paul or Alma (see Acts 9; Alma 36). But that is rare. Much more common is a quiet, gradual process, occurring over time, with an accompanying change of heart. Most of us get better gradually, without sensational manifestations. This statement by the prophet Joseph Smith explains: "We believe that the Holy Ghost is imparted by the laying on of hands of those in authority, and that the gift of the tongues, and also the gift of prophecy, are gifts of the spirit, and are obtained through that medium, but then to say that men always prophesied and spoke in tongues when they had the imposition of hands, would be to state that which is untrue, contrary to the practice of the Apostles, and at variance with holy writ; for Paul says, 'to one is given the gift of tongues, to another the gift of prophesy, and to another the gift of healing'—and again, 'do all prophecy? do all speak with tongues? do all interpret?' evidently shewing that all did not possess these several gifts, but that one received one gift and another received another gift—all did not prophecy; all did not speak in tongues; all did not work miracles; but all did receive the gift of the Holy Ghost; sometimes they spake in tongues and prophesied in the Apostles' days, and sometimes they did not.—The same is the case with us also in our administrations, *while more frequently there is no manifestation at all that is visible to the surrounding multitude*" (*Times and Seasons*, 3:823–24; emphasis added).

THE RESULTS OF BEING BORN AGAIN

Those who are born again have overcome the world. They have learned to bridle their passions and appetites. They have curbed every carnal and sensual desire. They stand valiantly for truth and righteousness. They fight the good fight of faith, denying themselves of all ungodliness. They are concerned about the building up of the kingdom of God, not in laying up in store the treasures of the earth. With them it is the kingdom of God or nothing. They use their talents in the service of others. They lay all they have upon the altar, consecrating all that God has blessed them with for the building up of Zion.

They who are born again have had a mighty change wrought in their hearts. They have become new creatures in Christ. They exercise faith in the redemptive power of Jesus. They are fully prepared to meet their Maker, willing to be judged according to their deeds in mortality. Their hearts are pure and their hands are clean of the blood and sins of their generation. Having been spiritually born of God, they receive God's image in their countenances. Though they still struggle with the trials and vicissitudes of life, they are on that straight and narrow way that leads to eternal glory in the celestial kingdom of God.

The Samaritan Woman at Jacob's Well
(John 4)

Nestled at the foot of Mount Gerizim, near the ancient city of Shechem in Samaria, there is a very old well. It is called Bir Ya'Qvb, Jacob's well. The great patriarch himself reportedly drank of the waters of the well, "and his children, and his cattle" (John 4:12). A Byzantine church was built on the site and rebuilt during the Crusades.

Jesus and his disciples, en route from Judea to Galilee, stopped by the well. The disciples went into the nearby village to purchase food, while Jesus, footsore and weary, stayed behind. We do not know if He rested in the shade of trees, which might have been growing near the well, or whether He sat on the stone parapet that would have surrounded the well itself.

A woman at the village came to fill her water jar, and Jesus said to her, "Give me to drink" (John 4:7).

The woman exclaimed in amazement, "How is it that thou, being a Jew, askest drink of me, which am a woman of Samaria? for the Jews have no dealings with the Samaritans" (John 4:9).

How right she was! Between the Jews and the Samaritans there existed bitter, long-standing hatred. The Samaritans claimed that Jacob was their father, and they were therefore entitled to be recognized as Israelites. But the Jews denied the claim; to them the Samaritans were a mongrel and heretic people, whose blood was mingled with that of the Assyrians and other heathen nations. The Jews so despised the Samaritans, to them an accursed and benighted people, that they sought ways to avoid even the most casual contact with Samaritans. True, food grown on Samaritan soil, or produced from Samaritan animals, was not, in and of itself, ritually unclean. But if Samaritan hands had touched the product, or processed it in any way, the food could not be eaten by a Jew. A Samaritan egg was clean, but not if it had been boiled by a Samaritan. Grapes or grain could be purchased by a Jew from a

Samaritan, but not wine or flour produced by Samaritan labor.

Jesus, who of course knew all about the enmity between Jews and Samaritans, did not respond with the contempt and derision common in Jewish-Samaritan communications. Rather, He used the opportunity to teach the woman, recognizing in her a soul in need of redemption.

"If thou knewest the gift of God, and who it is that saith to thee, Give me to drink; thou wouldest have asked of him, and he would have given thee living water" He said to her (John 4:10).

The woman had never heard of living water and must have been completely nonplused by Jesus' remark. All she knew was that if He wanted water to drink, it had to come from the well, which was deep (it is in fact 135 feet deep).

"Art thou greater than our father Jacob?" she asked. In other words, who do you think you are, anyway? Jesus continued His gentle teaching, perhaps gesturing toward the vessel with which she hauled water to the surface: "Whosoever drinketh of this water shall thirst again: but whosoever drinketh of the water that I shall give him shall never thirst; but the water that I shall give him shall be in him a well of water springing up into everlasting life" (John 4:12–14).

The woman, thinking perhaps that whatever it was He was offering would relieve her of the daily labor of drawing water, replied, "Sir, give me this water, that I thirst not, neither come hither to draw" (John 4:15).

The conversation continued. Jesus, knowing full well she had no current husband, though she was living with a man, asked her to call her husband to come and hear what He had to say. "I perceive thou art a prophet" (John 4:19), she replied, perhaps taken aback by how much He knew about her, a stranger. Jesus went on both to teach and correct her. "Ye worship ye know not what: . . . salvation is of the Jews. But the hour cometh, and now is, when the true worshippers shall worship the Father in spirit and in truth: for the Father seeketh such to worship him" (John 4:22–23).

The woman could only blurt out, "I know that

Messias cometh, which is called Christ: when he is come, he will tell us all things" (John 4:25).

This was the moment Jesus had been waiting for. In solemn grandeur He replied simply, "I that speak unto thee am he" (John 4:26). The language could not have been plainer. He, the mighty Jehovah, the supplier of living water, Lord of heaven and earth, revealed His true identity to a woman, and a Samaritan woman at that! No longer did she see Him as just another itinerant, a Jew passing through her country to Galilee.

Excitedly, she ran back to the village: "Come, see a man, which told me all things that ever I did: is not this the Christ?" (John 4:29).

This story is both interesting and instructive. It tells much about the democracy of heaven. Jesus had none of the bitter hostility and implacable rancor toward Samaritans held by the vast majority of Jews. Further, though a virtuous woman was honored and revered in Jewish society, the status of women was in no way equal to that of men. Yet Jesus, who loves everyone, fully accepted the Samaritan woman as His sister—not an inferior nor an enemy. She was hardly the cream of Samaritan society. For reasons unknown to us, she had had five husbands, and currently was living with another man, outside of marriage. She must have been on the very outer fringe of social respectability. But Jesus accepted her for what she was, with all her troubles. Thankfully, He does not demand perfection in those who come unto Him!

As was common with Him, Jesus saw something in the woman that warranted His attention. She had a believing heart. As their conversation progressed, she went from referring to Jesus as "a Jew," to "sir," to "a prophet," and finally as "the Christ." In a world that largely rejected Him, Jesus must have been gratified by her growing faith and acceptance. It gives me both hope and assurance that Jesus, who accepted a less-than-perfect Samaritan woman, will also accept me, with all of my faults and foibles.

Jesus' rejection of racism, which must be such a terrible affront to God and the curse of societies the world over, should remind all of the literal truth of the Apostle Paul's statement, uttered four decades after the episode at Jacob's well: God "hath made of one blood all nations of men for to dwell on all the face of the earth" (Acts 17:26). Only as we view all women everywhere as our sisters and all men as our brothers can we ever begin to bridge the gulf that keeps us apart from others because their race, gender, creed, or ethnicity is different than our own. In this, as in all other matters, Jesus is our exemplar, the template upon which we must build our own attitudes and actions.

Perhaps most significantly, the story teaches the importance of living water. The woman certainly knew, as does everyone else living in a desert land, that water is literally life-giving and life-sustaining. Without water, the thirsty traveler simply cannot survive. But she had to learn an even more basic lesson: weary wanderers through mortality hydrate their spirits by drinking from the wells of living water Jesus offers.

What then is "living water"? The answer is simple. Living water is the gospel of Christ, which speaks of Him and His atoning love. It is the message of salvation, which portrays Jesus as "the way, the truth and the life: no man cometh unto the Father, but by [Him]" (John 14:6). It is the life-giving spiritual refreshment and sustenance provided by the words of God's holy prophets in all ages. It is the ineffable joy that comes to those who keep Christ's commandments. "Unto him that keepeth my commandments," Jesus said, "I will give the mysteries of my kingdom, and the same shall be in him a well of living water, springing up unto everlasting life" (D&C 63:23).

FEEDING THE FIVE THOUSAND: PRELUDE TO THE BREAD OF LIFE SERMON

The third year of Jesus' public ministry began with a dramatic miracle—the feeding of five thousand from the content of a schoolboy's lunch. Jesus was preaching in Galilee. The Twelve had returned from their first missionary journey. Though undoubtedly tired physically, they reported to the Master "both what they had done, and what they had taught" (Mark 6:30). They found Him surrounded by multitudes of people, some attracted by His teachings, others because they saw in Him, or so they thought, a miracle worker who would deliver them from the oppression of Rome. Jesus, recognizing the apostles' need of rest and nourishment and their inability to receive either amidst the clamor of the crowd, said to the Twelve, "Come ye yourselves apart into a desert [i.e., solitary] place, and rest a while" (Mark 6:31). In search of a little peace and quiet, Jesus and the Twelve entered a boat and crossed the Sea of Galilee to a secluded rural spot near Bethsaida, on the eastern side of the lake. But they were not to have any privacy. Their departure had not been unnoticed. Many among the crowd saw Jesus and the Twelve depart and followed along the shore of the sea until they once more crowded around Him at the place where He had landed. Jesus, having compassion on them, taught them "many things" (Mark 6:34) and "healed their sick" (Matthew 14:14).

By now it was evening, and the crowd was hungry. The disciples said, "Send the multitude away, that they may go into the villages, and buy themselves victuals" (Matthew 14:15). Philip remarked that two hundred pennyworth (i.e., about 15 dollars) worth of bread would scarcely be enough to satisfy their hunger, and Andrew, another of the Twelve, noted there was a boy present who had five barley loaves and two small fishes, probably for his own evening meal. Jesus had the crowd sit down. Then He blessed the loaves and fishes and had His disciples distribute them among the crowd. When all had eaten He directed the remnants be collected. To their astonishment, twelve baskets full of uneaten fragments remained! The people exclaimed, "This is of a truth that prophet that should come into the world" (John 6:14). They tried to take Jesus by force, to make Him their king, but He, of course, demurred.

His disciples, so instructed by Jesus, departed across the sea toward Capernaum. Jesus remained behind to pray, the crowd having dispersed. He joined the disciples while they were yet at sea, walking upon the water in the midst of a terrible storm. Thomas Valetta has pointed out that the feeding of the five thousand was foreshadowed by the Israelites receiving manna in the wilderness; notes many parallels between the events recorded in John 6 and those surrounding the exodus of ancient Israel from Egypt (see *Ensign,* Mar. 1999, 7–13).

The boat carrying Jesus and the Twelve landed at morning somewhere on the shore of the plain of Gennesaret, a region on the northwestern side of the Sea of Galilee famed for its beauty and fertility. Word of His arrival soon spread to the villages throughout the region, and the people turned out in droves, to be taught and healed. Jesus and the Twelve, blessing and teaching, made their way toward Capernaum.

It was there, in the synagogue, that the crowd of the previous day, seeking another chance to have their bellies filled, found the Savior. They, too, had crossed the sea by boat. "Rabbi, when camest thou hither?" they inquired (John 6:25).

Jesus rebuked them. He knew full well what at least most of them wanted. In fairness, undoubtedly there were some who had come hungering and thirsting for the words of life and truth. But many, not recognizing in Jesus the *spiritual* Messiah Israel *needed,* clamored for the *temporal* Messiah Israel *wanted.* They wanted their bellies filled and the excitement of a "magic" show, which would demonstrate Jesus' earthly power. Bread *and* circuses.

In chastisement, Jesus proclaimed, "Ye seek me, not because ye saw the miracles, but because ye did eat of the loaves, and were filled. Labour not for the meat which perisheth, but for that meat which endureth unto everlasting life, which the Son of man shall give unto you" (John 6:26–27).

Interestingly, the Joseph Smith Translation of John 6:26 adds new insight to the reasons behind the Jews' seeking after Christ. It reads, "Ye seek me, not because ye desire to keep my sayings, neither because ye saw the miracles, but because ye did eat of the loaves, and were filled." Selfish physical desires, not spiritual hunger, motivated them.

Some of Jesus' listeners finally may have begun to grasp the difference between spiritual and physical food. "What shall we do," they asked, "that we might work the works of God?" (John 6:28).

Jesus, clearly revealing His true status as the Father's agent, replied, "This is the work of God, that ye believe on him whom he hath sent" (John 6:28).

But they wanted more. Give us a sign of your power, they demanded, reminding Jesus that God had given their forefathers manna from heaven while the Israelites sojourned in the desert. Only something as unusual, as spectacular, as manna had been would satisfy them.

Their words illustrate the problem with sign-seekers. Signs alone never satisfy. Big demands bigger; yesterday's sign is soon forgotten. Foolish as they were, many of Jesus' questioners seemed already to have forgotten the miracle of only the previous day, when five thousand had been fed on a few bites of bread and fish.

THE BREAD OF LIFE

Jesus did not permit the reference to manna to go unchallenged. "Moses gave you not that bread from heaven; but my Father giveth you the true bread from heaven. For the bread of God is he which cometh down from heaven, and giveth life unto the world." He continued, clearly attesting His messianic status, "I am the bread of life: he that cometh to me shall never hunger; and he that believeth on me shall never thirst" (John 6:32, 35).

Few of Jesus' listeners could have misunderstood what He said. They all knew that bread is the very staff of life. Indeed, bread, or at least the wheat from which it is made, provided the basis for Western civilization itself. J. Bronowski has pointed out that the largest single step in the ascent of man is the change from nomad to village agriculture. That step was made possible by the appearance of bread wheat in ancient Mesopotamia perhaps 9000 years ago. The availability of wheat meant that everyone no longer had to spend all day, every day, hunting and gathering. People could congregate in villages, and specialization of labor became possible. Wheat, and the water needed to grow it and convert it into bread, make civilization possible. Bronowski also noted that the presence of water in a desert oasis turned a barren hillside into Jericho, the oldest city in the world (see *The Ascent of Man*).

Jesus' questioners knew at least the basic elements of that story: bread is the stuff of civilization and the staff of life. Furthermore, the Jews, with their long rabbinical tradition, were skilled in allegory and verbal imagery. They knew full well what Jesus meant when he said, "I am the bread of life."

But the Jews still professed unbelief or, perhaps more correctly, unwillingness to believe. A common way to reject an unwanted message is to reject the messenger. This they tried to do: Isn't this man, with his high-flown ideas about being the bread sent down from heaven, just the son of Joseph, whose father and mother we know? Who does he think he is, anyway?

Jesus repeated His assertion: "I am that bread of life. Your fathers did eat manna in the wilderness, and are dead. This is the bread which cometh down from heaven, that a man may eat thereof, and not die" (John 6:48–50).

He shocked His listeners even further: "The bread that I will give is my flesh" (John 6:51). They turned away in disgust. How *dare* He speak like that! They were no cannibals! But Jesus pressed on: "Except ye eat the flesh of the Son of man, and drink his blood, ye have no life in you. Whoso eateth my flesh, and drinketh my blood, hath eternal life; and I will raise him up at the last day. For my flesh is meat indeed, and my blood is drink indeed" (John 6:53–55).

That was more than most of the crowd could stand. They had had enough of this "hard saying." Unwilling to even try to understand what Jesus was saying, they drifted away, and "walked no more with Him" (John 6:66).

Jesus asked of the Twelve, in what was one of the biggest tests of their ministry, "Will ye also go away?"

Peter, on behalf of the others, replied, "Lord, to whom shall we go? Thou hast the words of eternal life. And we believe and are sure that thou art that Christ, the Son of the living God" (John 6:67–69). The Twelve had passed the test. At least partially, they grasped the spiritual significance of Jesus' assertion.

What did Jesus mean when He spoke of the need to eat His flesh and drink His blood if we are to have eternal life? Clearly, His expression was not to be taken literally, but figuratively. He becomes the Bread of Life—the giver of eternal life, to all who accept Him as their redeeming Savior. To worthily eat the flesh and drink the blood of Jesus, figuratively speaking, is to accept Him completely and without reservation as the Christ of God. It signifies our willingness to always remember Him, to keep His commandments, and to take upon ourselves His sacred name. We do so through the sacred ordinance of the sacrament.

We partake of the sacrament—or we should—to satisfy our spiritual hunger, signify our resolution to repent of our sins, renew our covenants with God, and commune with Jesus Christ. Sad to say, some there are who view the sacramental experience only as a perfunctory exercise, a sterile ritual, which they go through without really thinking about it too much. How many times have you noted the giggling teenagers, the whispering adults exchanging confidences, the elders quorum teacher reviewing his lesson while the sacrament is being blessed and passed? In contrast, who can ever forget those sacrament services when the air seemed thick with the Spirit, when the audience, collectively and individually, seemed transported to a higher plane of spirituality, when all communed with the Divine?

In his usual direct way, President Brigham Young

addressed the problem of perfunctory observance of the sacramental ordinance. He said, "In [the sacrament] we here attend to . . . we show to the Father that we remember . . . Jesus Christ, . . . that we are willing to take upon us his name. When we are doing this, *I want the minds here as well as the bodies. I want the whole man here when you come to meeting*" (*Discourses of Brigham Young,* 171; emphasis added).

HOW OFTEN SHOULD WE PARTAKE OF THE SACRAMENT?

In most Christian churches, the sacrament is administered to the congregation only infrequently, usually at Christmas and Easter. Latter-day Saints, on the other hand, believe the sacrament should be partaken of every week. Elder Melvin J. Ballard explains: "Who is there among us that does not wound his spirit by word, thought, or deed, from Sabbath to Sabbath? We do things for which we are sorry and desire to be forgiven, or we have erred against someone and given injury. If there is a feeling in our hearts that we are sorry for what we have done, if there is a feeling in our souls that we would like to be forgiven, then the method to obtain forgiveness is not through rebaptism; it is not to make confession to man; but it is to repent of our sins, to go to those against whom we have sinned or transgressed and obtain their forgiveness and then repair to the sacrament table where, if we have sincerely repented and put ourselves in proper condition, we shall be forgiven, and spiritual healing will come to our souls. . . . I am a witness that there is a spirit attending the administration of the sacrament that warms the soul from head to foot; you feel the wounds of the spirit being healed, and the load being lifted. Comfort and happiness come to the soul that is worthy and truly desirous of partaking of this spiritual food" (*Melvin J. Ballard—Crusader for Righteousness*, 132–33).

In summary, Jesus is both the Living Water and the Bread of Life. "Come and see": You will find that He provides the spiritual nourishment required for the growth of your spirit and the healing of your soul.

The symbolism of Jesus as Living Water and Bread of Life gives added meaning to this assertion that He also is the Light and Life of the world.

CHAPTER FOUR

COME AND SEE . . .
THE LIGHT AND LIFE
OF THE WORLD

The Lord is my light, my all and in all.
There is in his sight no darkness at all.
He is my Redeemer, my Savior, and King.
With Saints and with angels his praises I'll sing.
HYMNS, NO. 89

In chapter two, we dealt with Jesus' reaction to the woman taken in adultery. That scene took place within the temple enclosure, in a colonnaded court-yard known as the Court of the Women. Jesus moved to another part of the temple enclosure, a building known as the Treasury, where He continued His teaching. Readers will recall these events took place at the end of the Feast of Tabernacles, a festive time in the Jewish year. Lamps celebrating the joyous occasion lighted the courtyard. Perhaps gesturing toward them, Jesus, the Master Teacher, who used simple examples to illustrate celestial principles, declared: "I am the light of the world: he that followeth me shall not walk in darkness, but shall have the light of life" (John 8:12).

True to form, the Pharisees disputed His words. "Thou bearest record of thyself; thy record is not true." In other words, how can we trust the testimony of someone who is his own witness?

Jesus replied: "Though I bear record of myself, yet my record is true: for I know whence I came, and whither I go. . . . If I judge, my judgment is true: for I am not alone, but I and the Father that sent me. . . . I am one that bear witness of myself, and the Father that sent me beareth witness of me" (John 8:14–18). Note the complete and perfect unity between Jesus and His Father. Together they constituted the two witnesses required by Jewish law to determine questions of guilt or innocence (see Deuteronomy 17:6).

The Pharisees, though they would not accept Jesus for what He was, surely knew full well the messianic prophecies of Isaiah, who described the Savior-to-come as "a light to the Gentiles" and God's "salvation unto the end of the earth" (Isaiah 49:6).

Speaking of a time yet future, Isaiah had proclaimed to Israel, "Arise, shine; for thy light is come, and the glory of the Lord is risen upon thee. For behold, the darkness shall cover the earth, and gross darkness the people: but the Lord shall arise upon thee . . . and the Gentiles shall come to thy light" (Isaiah 60:1–3). All this the Pharisees no doubt knew, yet still they sought to take Jesus' life. But "no man laid hands on him; for his hour was not yet come" (John 8:20).

In proclaiming Himself the Light of the World, Jesus drew a dramatic distinction between light and darkness. Those two are in direct opposition to each other. They cannot exist together. Where there is light, darkness is banished. If darkness descends, light disappears. Light commonly is equated in the scriptures with love, righteousness, understanding, wisdom, happiness, and other attributes of godliness. Darkness, on the other hand, is used in the scriptures to describe corruption, evil, ignorance, and wickedness. In spiritual terms, one is of God, the other of the devil. Scriptural examples make the point:

LIGHT

- "Thy word [i.e., God's word] is a lamp unto my feet, and a light unto my path" (Psalm 119:105).
- "O house of Jacob, come ye, and let us walk in the light of the Lord" (Isaiah 2:5).
- "Light and understanding and excellent wisdom is found in thee" (Daniel 5:14).
- "Let your light so shine before men, that they may see your good works, and glorify your Father which is in heaven" (Matthew 5:16).
- "Let us put on the armour of light" (Romans 13:12).
- "That which is of God is light; and he that receiveth light, and continueth in God, receiveth more light; and that light groweth brighter and brighter until the perfect day" (D&C 50:24).

DARKNESS

- "The way of the wicked *is* as darkness: they know not at what they stumble" (Proverbs 4:19).
- "But he that hateth his brother is in darkness" (1 John 2:10–11).
- "And have no fellowship with the unfruitful works

of darkness, but rather reprove them" (Ephesians 5:11).

- "And that which doth not edify is not of God, and is darkness" (D&C 50:23).
- "Watch, for the adversary spreadeth his dominions, and darkness reigneth" (D&C 82:5).

JESUS, THE BRINGER OF LIGHT

Jesus' birth was—literally—a glorious celebration of light. The Book of Mormon records that "there was no darkness in all that night, but it was as light as though it was mid-day. . . . the sun did rise in the morning again, according to its proper order; and they knew that it was the day that the Lord should be born, because of the sign which had been given" (3 Nephi 1:19). After Christ's crucifixion, in contrast, when the prince of darkness fancied he had won, "there was thick darkness upon all the face of the land, insomuch that the inhabitants thereof who had not fallen could feel the vapor of darkness; and there could be no light" (3 Nephi 8:20–21).

Peter spoke of Christ "who hath called you out of darkness into his marvellous light" (1 Peter 2:9).

From the darkness of disbelief, ignorance, and sin, He calls us into the "marvelous light" of love, forgiveness, mercy, and understanding. Open the eyes of your understanding, and see me, He says, in effect. "Behold, I am Jesus Christ, . . . a light which cannot be hid in darkness" (D&C 14:9). In effect He says to all: I will shine my light into every corner of your character. I will take away your sins if you will but come to me. Nothing can separate you from my love. No matter how much darkness has clouded and corroded your soul, I will cleanse you and heal you. I will bring light and truth into your life. Behold, I stand at the door and knock. Please let me enter.

Paul wrote, "For God, who commanded the light to shine out of darkness, hath shined in our hearts, to *give* the light of the knowledge of the glory of God in the face of Jesus Christ" (2 Corinthians 4:6). Jesus is "the light which shineth in darkness" (D&C 6:21).

Members of my family and I were in France in 1999 when a total eclipse of the sun occurred. As the moment approached, the darkness deepened, until there came the time when the sun was completely blotted out, and total darkness reigned.

Then, slowly at first, but with accelerating effect, the sun reappeared, and life came back to the earth. As much as I understood the science involved, it was still a frightening experience.

So it is with all of us. If we permit the powers of darkness to prevail in our lives, light retreats. Eventually, unless we change our ways, there will be no light, and the prince of darkness will be in complete charge of us. But if we permit the sun (or rather, the Son of God) to enter our lives, darkness will be driven away, slowly at first, but finally totally and completely as we give ourselves fully to Him.

Light is always associated with Deity. At the glorious First Vision, the prophet Joseph Smith saw "a pillar of light exactly over my head, above the brightness of the sun. . . . When the light rested upon me I saw two Personages, whose brightness and glory defy all description, standing above me in the air. One of them spake unto me, calling me by name and said, pointing to the other—*This is My Beloved Son. Hear Him!* (JS–H 1:16–17; italics in the original).

The resurrected Jesus is also a being of light. In a wondrous vision of Christ manifested to Joseph

Smith and Oliver Cowdery in the Kirtland Temple on April 3, 1836, the Savior is described as follows: "His eyes were as a flame of fire; the hair of his head was white like the pure snow; His countenance shone above the brightness of the sun" (D&C 110:3).

Jesus, the Bringer of Light, illuminates the truth of all things for us. Indeed, He is both the light *and* the truth. As such, He is the fullness of all that man can even aspire to emulate, the sum and more of human existence, the farthest reach of human potential. The more light we receive from Him, the more we understand and accept the truth. As we gain access to more truth, we receive more light, and that "light groweth brighter and brighter until the perfect day" (D&C 50:24). In other words, if we will but pay the price we can receive that fullness of light that circumscribes and encompasses all truth. Only then can we become as He is (see 3 Nephi 27:27).

To do so is the task of the eternities. The prophet Joseph Smith explained: "When you climb up a lad-der, you must begin at the bottom, and ascend step by step, until you arrive at the top; and so it is with the principles of the gospel—you must begin with the first, and go on until you learn all the principles of exaltation. But it will be a great while after you have passed through the veil before you will have learned them. It is not all to be comprehended in this world; it will be a great work to learn our salvation and exaltation even beyond the grave" (*History of the Church,* 6:306–7).

THE LIGHT OF CHRIST

There is a spirit, known by various names, including the light of Christ, the light of truth, or the spirit of Christ, which pervades every corner of the universe. It is everywhere, proceeding forth from the presence of God to fill the immensity of space. It is the power by which the earth and all else in the universe was made.

The light of Christ is not a personage. It has no form or shape. It is not the Holy Ghost, though the Holy Ghost uses it for His purposes, to bless and comfort God's children. We know little about the nature of the light of Christ save that it exists and is the light of truth, "the light which is in all things, which giveth life to all things, . . . the law by which all things are governed, even the power of God" (D&C 88:13). It is "the true light that lighteth every man that cometh into the world" (D&C 93:2). Were it not present, life would cease. One of its manifestations is called conscience. By it the Lord guides the affairs of men and directs the courses of nations. By it the Lord gives to man the discoveries of science and the arts. It governs the human creative process in all of its myriad manifestations. President Brigham Young spoke of the role of intelligence, or in other words, "light and truth" (D&C 93:36), in the enlightenment of the human mind: "It is not the optic nerve alone that gives the knowledge of surrounding objects to the mind, but it is that which God has placed in man—a system of intelligence that attracts knowledge, as light cleaves to light, intelligence to intelligence, and truth to truth. It is this which lays in man a proper foundation for all education" (*Discourses of Brigham Young*, 257).

Those who experience that process of enlightenment—whether as "pure intelligence flowing into you" (*Teachings of the Prophet Joseph Smith*, 151) or as new insight, which enables one to visualize something in a new light, as for the first time—act under the influence of the light of Christ. That light illuminates truth, enabling man to see things as they really are. Under its influence our "eyes [are] opened and our understandings [are] enlightened" (D&C 76:12). The poet Wordsworth expressed those feelings thusly: "And I have felt a presence that disturbs me with the joy / Of elevated thoughts; a sense sublime / Of something far more deeply interfused, / Whose dwelling is the light of setting suns" ("Lines Composed a Few Miles above Tintern Abbey").

You Cannot Live on Borrowed Light

Many there are, sad to say, who lose conviction or even interest in Christ and His gospel under the pressures of ridicule or opposition. Having "tasted of the fruit they [are] ashamed, because of those that [are] scoffing at them; and they [fall] away into forbidden paths" (1 Nephi 8:28). Like the seed that falls on stony places in the parable of the sower (see Matthew 13:3–9, 18–23), they lack a faith sufficient to sustain them.

Well over a century ago, President Heber C. Kimball prophesied of a time to come when the faith of the Saints would be challenged in difficult and trying ways. His prescient pronouncement is of increasing importance for the Church in our day, a time when men call good evil, and evil good (see Isaiah 5:20), a time when the adversary reigns in the hearts of many. "Let me say to you," said President Kimball, "that many of you will see the time when you will have all the trouble, trial and persecution that you can stand, and plenty of opportunities to show that you are true to God and his work. This Church has before it many close places through which it will have to pass before the work of God is crowned with victory. To meet the difficulties that are coming, it will be necessary for you to have a knowledge of the truth of this work for yourselves. The difficulties will be of such a character that the man or woman who does not possess this personal knowledge or witness will fall. If you have not got the testimony, live right and call upon the Lord and cease not till you obtain it. If you do not you will not stand.

"Remember these sayings, for many of you will

live to see them fulfilled. The time will come when no man nor woman will be able to endure on borrowed light. Each will have to be guided by the light within himself. If you do not have it, how can you stand?

". . . You will be left to the light within yourselves. If you don't have it you will not stand; therefore seek for the testimony of Jesus and cleave to it, that when the trying time comes you may not stumble and fall" (*Life of Heber C. Kimball*, 449–50).

JESUS HEALS BOTH SPIRITUAL AND PHYSICAL BLINDNESS

Jesus banishes spiritual darkness and heals our souls of spiritual blindness. During His earthly ministry He also brought sight to many who were literally blind by reason of affliction, disease, or accident. One such miracle is described in John, chapter 9. (Since John is the only gospel writer on this matter, it is probable he actually witnessed it.)

The Feast of Tabernacles was over. Jesus, for the moment, had escaped those who sought His life. As He and His disciples walked through the streets of

Jerusalem, on the Sabbath, it is likely they passed by many scenes of the recent festivities—discarded decorations, abandoned booths, the stubs of burned-out candles. Whatever else Jesus encountered, John records that as He passed by, Jesus "saw a man which was blind from his birth" (John 9:1). The scriptures indicate that the man was a beggar, one of many who eked out a precarious existence on whatever pittance others were prepared to put in his outstretched hand. How typical of Jesus that He would notice the human wreckage such as is found on the streets of every big city. Unlike most of us, who hurry along, trying hard not to look at others on the crowded streets, perhaps annoyed at the sights and sounds and odors of those looking for a handout, Jesus noticed everyone and was interested in everyone. He stopped, His compassion raised by the poor creature with blank face and vacant, unseeing eyes.

His disciples evidently assumed that sin was the cause of the man's affliction and that God was punishing him. How often do we, with our own spiritual short-sightedness, suppose that someone's plight is the result of God's punishing him or her?

How often do we unjustly blame our own personal misfortune on nonexistent sin? I know a good woman, the wife of a dear friend, and mother of a large family. When her children were young, they, like most other children, brought home numerous upper respiratory viruses acquired at school. The mother, seeing one or more of her children with a minor illness, was convinced that somehow, somewhere, someone in the family had sinned and that God was punishing them. Not likely; being a Christian doesn't exempt us from the effects of germ-caused diseases!

No, it's not that simple. In the case of the blind man, it was, of course, conceivable that he might indeed have been born blind because of his parents' sins. Individual wickedness and resultant diseases can and do bring bodily affliction to self or others. But we must be very reluctant to draw firm conclusions about situations about which we usually know very little. The all-too-human tendency to jump to conclusions, to ascribe guilt where there is none, to prematurely judge the ultimate cause of misfortune, must be avoided. President N. Eldon Tanner pointed out the difficulties of rendering righteous judgment. He said, "When we try to judge people, which we should not do, we have a great tendency to look for and take pride in finding weaknesses and faults, such as vanity, dishonesty, immorality, and intrigue. As a result, we see only the worst side of those being judged" ("Judge Not, That Ye Be Not Judged," *Ensign,* July 1972, 35).

Jesus settled the question of culpability with one sentence: "Neither hath this man sinned, nor his parents: but that the works of God should be made manifest in him" (John 9:3). In other words, the man's blindness had occurred so that the work and power of God might be shown in his life. Ask yourself, if you will, whether such might also apply to you. Might your own misfortune or limitation—be it physical, intellectual, emotional, or whatever—be an opportunity for God to use *your* life as an occasion to display Himself to others?

The Apostle Paul may have come to that understanding. He suffered, chronically, from something that he termed "a thorn in the flesh, the messenger of Satan to buffet me" (2 Corinthians 12:7). Commentators on Paul's life have speculated on the nature of his affliction. Was it chronic malaria, some other long-standing disease, or was it, as Richard Lloyd Anderson suggests, one of Paul's bitter opponents who attacked him and the doctrine he espoused? (See *Understanding Paul,* 141–42). We simply don't know. But whatever it was, Paul besought the Lord thrice "that it might depart from me." He received this reply from Deity: "My grace is sufficient for thee: for my strength is made perfect in weakness." Paul concluded, "Most gladly therefore will I rather glory in my infirmities, that the power of Christ may rest upon me" (2 Corinthians 12:7–9).

But back to our story of Jesus and the blind man. Jesus, again using an actual event to teach an eternal principle, and recognizing the state of the poor wretch who had been in darkness from his birth, declared again, "I am the light of the world" (John 9:5). Then He anointed the blind man's eyes with moistened clay, and told him to go and wash in the pool of Siloam. The man did so, and miracle of miracles, *he could see!* In a moment he saw for the first time the blue of the sky, his own fingers, the sparkle of the sun, the trees and flowers. What a glorious miracle had happened to him! The curtain of darkness, which had been his constant companion all of his days, was lifted in an instant. Jesus had actually created sight, not restored it. After all, the man had been born blind. We can only imagine his excitement as he ran home to tell his parents what had happened. No longer did he have to feel his way along, stumbling and falling over every obstacle in his path. He could run, carefree, avoiding other pedestrians, street litter, children playing, stray dogs, whatever was in his way.

The nowsighted man's joy was, however, short-lived. The neighbors first couldn't believe their own eyes. Is this really the man who "sat and begged," they asked. It looks like him, but how can it be? The man reassured them of his identity and in reply to their question, "How were thine eyes opened?" replied, "A man that is called Jesus made clay, and anointed mine eyes, and said unto me, go . . . and wash: and I went and washed, and I received sight" (John 9:10–11). The Pharisees questioned the man, but could not shake his simple story. They then tried to bully his parents, who shrugged off their questions: "We know that this is our son, and that he was born blind: but by what means he now seeth, we know not; or who hath opened his eyes, we know not: he is of age; ask him: he shall speak for himself" (John 9:20–21). The Pharisees again questioned the man, trying to get him to condemn Jesus as a Sabbath-breaking sinner. He again refused, commenting: "Now we know that God heareth not sinners: but if any man be a worshipper of God, and doeth his will, him he heareth. Since the world began was it not heard that any man opened the eyes of one that was born blind. If this man were not of God, he could do nothing" (John 9:31–33). In their rage and frustration, the Pharisees threw the man out of the synagogue. In our parlance, they excommunicated him.

Jesus, having heard of this deplorable state of affairs, sought out the man and asked him, "Dost thou believe on the Son of God? He answered and said, Who is he, Lord, that I might believe on him? And Jesus said unto him, Thou hast both seen him, and it is he that talketh with thee." (In reading this conversation, recorded in John 9:35–37, recall that the only other time Jesus had conversed with the man was before he had received his sight. The man had therefore never seen Jesus until this moment.)

The man, convinced by the sight of the Personage who stood before him, and hearing the voice he would never forget, cried out, "Lord, I believe" (John 9:38) and worshipped Jesus.

The underlying principle involved in this matter was, of course, not lost on Jesus. He said, both in sadness and in condemnation, that he had "come into this world, that they which see not might see; and that they which see might be made blind" (John 9:39). To the Pharisee's query, "Are we blind also?" Jesus replied simply: "If ye were blind, ye should have no sin: but now ye say, We see; therefore your sin remaineth" (John 9:40–41). Though, in His compassion, He gave sight to the man blind since birth, the Savior was much more concerned with the spiritual blindness of those who, having eyes, would not see.

"Let Your Light so Shine . . ."

In the Sermon on the Mount, which has been called "the constitution for a perfect life" (Harold B.

Lee, *Decisions for Successful Living*, 57), Jesus counseled, "Let your light so shine before men, that they may see your good works, and glorify your Father which is in heaven" (Matthew 5:16). What is that light? Is it the light of faith? Yes. But is it also the light of righteous service to others, of keeping the Lord's commandments? Yes. Does shining that light include partaking of the saving ordinances of the gospel? Yes, indeed.

Christ spoke of our need to show others our good works, not for the purposes of self-aggrandizement, but to glorify God. Good works, then, are important.

Some other Christians reject the Latter-day Saint view that salvation comes from both grace and works. They point for support to Ephesians 2:8, where Paul writes, "For by grace are ye saved through faith; and that not of yourselves: it is the gift of God." Latter-day Saints do not dispute that position, though we believe more explanation is required if one is to properly understand the relationship between grace and works. As are so many other doctrines, this one is illuminated by the Book of

Mormon: "It is by grace that we are saved, *after all we can do*" (2 Nephi 25:23; emphasis added).

Latter-day Saints have thus been given to know that to be saved, every individual must come unto Christ, be born again through His atonement, and become His spiritual offspring. A Nephite prophet, King Benjamin, provided this explanation: "And now, because of the covenant which ye have made ye shall be called the children of Christ, his sons, and his daughters; for behold, this day he hath spiritually begotten you; for ye say that your hearts are changed through faith on his name; therefore, ye are born of him and have become his sons and his daughters. And under this head ye are made free, and . . . there is no other name given whereby salvation cometh; therefore, I would that ye should take upon you the name of Christ, all you that have entered into the covenant with God that ye should be obedient unto the end of your lives" (Mosiah 5:7–8).

Note that we are to come to Christ, take His name upon us, become His spiritual sons and daughters, and "be obedient unto the end of [our] lives" (Mosiah 5:8). If we do so, His grace is sufficient for our salvation, despite our mortal weaknesses. These additional words from the Book of Mormon come to mind: "My grace is sufficient for all men that humble themselves before me; for if they humble themselves before me, and have faith in me, then will I make weak things become strong unto them" (Ether 12:27).

If we live dissolute, profligate, wicked lives, can we fall back upon the grace of Christ as sufficient to redeem us? Not in the view of the Latter-day Saints. We show our love for Christ, and our willingness to follow Him, by the extent to which we keep His commandments. "He that hath my commandments and keepeth them," Jesus said, "he it is that loveth me" (John 14:21).

Part of keeping the commandments is partaking worthily of the sacred gospel ordinances. We cannot be redeemed without the ordinances. They are crucial. We show our faith *by* our works, not *despite* them, or *without* them (see James 2:14–18)

Strive as we will, and must, however, we still fall short of being able to earn or deserve the blessings of God. Based on our own efforts, as essential as those are, we remain indebted to God's grace. "If ye should serve him with all your whole souls yet ye would be unprofitable servants" (Mosiah 2:21). But we must strive, with all our hearts, to keep His commandments, enduring to the end of our days, if we are to receive the full force of Christ's atonement in our lives. We cannot earn salvation by our individual works—to think otherwise would be to dethrone Christ as our Savior—but we must "try his works to do," (*Hymns,* no. 194) as a token of our good faith and to demonstrate our willingness to keep the covenant we have entered into to be obedient to God. Thus, for Latter-day Saints it is not a matter of "grace alone" or "works alone." A balance between the two is required, both being essential.

"Come and see," and you will find that living without Him was like living in perpetual twilight. As you bask in His light, you will find power, strength, and growing understanding coming to you, and you will see and live as never before.

We have already noted many examples of Jesus' supernal capacity as a teacher of truth. We shall now examine that concept in more detail.

CHAPTER FIVE

COME AND SEE . . . THE MASTER TEACHER

Teach me to walk in the light of his love;
Teach me to pray to my Father above;
Teach me to know of the things that are right;
Teach me, teach me to walk in the light.

HYMNS, NO. 304

In His mortal ministry, Jesus was, above all else, a teacher. Indeed, the term *rabbi,* (*teacher*) is used to describe Him no less than sixty times in the four Gospels. But Jesus was more than an ordinary teacher, and greater than a master teacher: He was *the* teacher, unequaled in His ability to touch and change the hearts and minds of His listeners. In this He stands alone, unchallenged. But it must be understood that although Jesus' teaching was superb in every way, it was not an end in itself, but rather the means by which He accomplished His divinely appointed mission.

Furthermore, Jesus utilized many teaching methods throughout His ministry, varying them, in His infinite wisdom, according to the audience and circumstances.

Jesus' teachings, simple yet profound, were at the same time both comforting and disturbing. He often taught in ways that both revealed and concealed important spiritual truths. Many scholars consider Jesus to be the originator of the widespread use of parables as a mode of instruction. Parables are stories depicting true-to-life events used to illustrate a moral or spiritual lesson. Jesus used them extensively in His teaching. There are, for example, seven parables found in Matthew 13. All of them, as the prophet Joseph Smith pointed out (*Teachings of the Prophet Joseph Smith*, 94), relate to the gathering of Israel—the process whereby the scattered descendants of Israel are contacted gradually, wherever they are to be found around the globe, and invited to receive the blessings of the gospel. The first of the seven parables in Matthew 13 is the majestic parable of the sower, which deals with the planting of the gospel seed. The concluding parable, the parable of the net, tells of the final sorting and severing of the wicked from the righteous.

Why did Jesus use parables so extensively in His teaching? He explained: "Because it is given unto you [the disciples] to know the mysteries of the kingdom of heaven, but to them [the unbelievers] it is not given. For whosoever hath, to him shall be given, and he shall have more abundance: but whosoever hath not, from him shall be taken away even that he hath. Therefore speak I to them in parables: because they seeing see not; and hearing they hear not, neither do they understand" (Matthew 13:11–13). The spiritually attuned will understand the deep spiritual message of the simple story told in a parable, but others, they who "seeing see not," will not understand. Had Jesus always taught plain, unvarnished truth, readily discernible to all, many of his hearers would have come under condemnation. They were too weak in faith and unprepared in heart to accept and obey the words of saving truth.

Parables always contain a living kernel of gospel truth within the seed-coat of a simple tale. Through careful and prayerful analysis the truth may be discerned. Since the setting of the parables always dealt with familiar episodes from daily life, those who heard them would have opportunities, as they went about their daily tasks, not only to remember the parable, but to ponder and contemplate its spiritual meaning, thus multiplying the impact of the story in the lives of the listeners.

Those who wish to emulate the Master's teaching style, recognizing their best efforts inevitably will fall short, of course, can do nothing better than simply read, strive to understand, and teach with plainness the doctrines and spiritual lessons found in the Gospels. As President Boyd K. Packer has said, they (the Gospels) "constitute a treatise on teaching technique surpassed by none" (*Teach Ye Diligently*, 23).

What made Jesus such a superb teacher, *the* Master Teacher of all time? There are many answers, including the following:

LOVE

An effective teacher of moral principles and spiritual truths must love both the message and the audience. Jesus excelled in both respects. With regard to the message, Jesus knew and used effectively the scriptures and the words of earlier prophets to ask and answer questions, explain parables, and prophesy of His own betrayal and death. He even used scriptures (see Matthew 4:1–11) to thwart Satan when tempted by the adversary! An interesting episode at the very beginning of Jesus' ministry illustrates how effectively He was able to "bridge" between earlier prophets and Himself.

Jesus was in Nazareth, where he had been reared. Now grown to manhood, He went into the synagogue on the Sabbath day, as He had done so many times as boy and man. At the point in the service where the scriptures were to be read to the congregation, the rabbi in charge handed Jesus the book of Isaiah, which would have been in the form of a scroll. Jesus found the place we know as Isaiah 61:1–2 and read: "The Spirit of the Lord is upon me; because he hath anointed me to preach the gospel to the poor; he hath sent me to heal the broken-hearted, to preach deliverance to the captives, and recovering of sight to the blind, to set at liberty them that are bruised." He then sat down, under the gaze of all who were present. Then Jesus spake, revealing His true identity: "This day is this scripture fulfilled in your ears" (Luke

4:18–19, 21). To say the least the audience was startled. "Is not this Joseph's son?" they asked, proving the adage Jesus Himself quoted, "No prophet is accepted in his own country" (Luke 4:22, 24).

Jesus spoke and taught the doctrines of His Father. In so doing, He manifested His total submission to the will of the Father. "My doctrine is not mine," He said, "but his that sent me. If any man will do his will, he shall know of the doctrine, whether it be of God, or whether I speak of myself. He that speaketh of himself seeketh his own glory: but he that seeketh his glory that sent him, the same is true, and no unrighteousness is in him" (John 7:16–18).

On another occasion Jesus said, "For I have not spoken of myself; but the Father which sent me, he gave me a commandment, what I should say, and what I should speak" (John 12:49).

Jesus loved the doctrine that He preached, just as He loved the Father whose doctrine it was. Such is the unity between Father and Son, that the doctrine was Jesus' doctrine equally as it was that of the Father. Recall the words of the resurrected Savior to the Nephites: "Behold I have given unto you my gospel, and this is the gospel which I have given unto you—that I came into the world to do the will of my Father, because my Father sent me. And my Father sent me that I might be lifted up upon the cross; . . . that I might draw all men unto me . . . to be judged of their works. . . . Whoso repenteth and is baptized in my name shall be filled; and if he endureth to the end, behold, him will I hold guiltless before my Father. . . . nothing entereth into his rest save it be those who have washed their garments in my blood" (3 Nephi 27:13–21).

Jesus loved those whom He taught, completely and without reservation. Even those who rejected Him, abused Him, and eventually betrayed and killed Him were loved wholeheartedly. Who can ever forget His words on the cross concerning the Roman soldiers who had crucified and were putting Him to death: "Father, forgive them; for they know not what they do" (Luke 23:34)? Jesus simply could not hate another; it was impossible for Him to do so. His very nature forbade it. Nor did He turn away those who had rejected Him. Of them He said: "Unto such shall ye continue to minister; for ye know not but what they will return and repent, and come unto me with full purpose of heart, and I shall heal them" (3 Nephi 18:32).

Part of loving people is to trust them and to see in them the ability to stretch and grow spiritually. That is what Jesus did. As President Spencer W. Kimball said, "Jesus knew how to involve his disciples in the process of life. He gave them important and specific things to do for their development. Other leaders have sought to be so omnicompetent that they have tried to do everything themselves, which produces little growth in others. Jesus trusts his followers enough to share his work with them so that they can grow. . . . Jesus gave people truths and tasks that were matched to their capacity. He did not overwhelm them with more than they could manage, but gave them enough to stretch their souls" (*The Teachings of Spencer W. Kimball*, 482).

EXAMPLE

Jesus taught as He lived. In each and every aspect of life He was the perfect Exemplar of Truth. The example of His sinless, perfect life is the greatest sermon He ever gave. As President David O. McKay said:

"We teach more by what we are and do than by what we say: we teach by contagion. So it was with Jesus. The eloquence of His words is cold in contrast with the warmth of his personality. He taught by what he was and what he did" (*Pathways to Happiness,* 278–79).

If it be true that a teacher is no greater as a teacher than he or she is as a person, Jesus was the perfect teacher—because He was a perfect person. His teachings have their greatest meaning, not because He said, "Love one another" (John 15:12), but because He showed His love by giving His life a ransom for all; not because He said, "Blessed are the peacemakers" (Matthew 5:9), but because He is the Prince of Peace; not because He said, "Love your enemies, bless them that curse you" (Matthew 5:44), but because on Calvary's cruel cross He asked the Father to forgive the tormentors who would take His sinless life (see Luke 23:34). It was from Jesus that the Twelve learned to teach by example.

PRAYER

Jesus was in almost constant communion with His Father. Every major decision He made was preceded by heartfelt prayer. Before He called His twelve apostles, He "went out into a mountain to pray, and continued all night in prayer to God. And when it was day, he called unto him his disciples: and of them he chose twelve, whom also he named apostles" (Luke 6:12–13). In the greatest sermon ever given, He taught us how to pray, in that sublime example we know as the Lord's Prayer (Matthew 6:9–13). In the hour of His greatest agony of mind and spirit, He poured out His heart in humble supplication to the Father: "O my Father, if it be possible, let this cup pass from me: nevertheless not as I will, but as thou wilt" (Matthew 26:39). Then, though He had sweat great drops of blood in His incomprehensible suffering (see Luke 22:44; D&C 19:18), He arose to His feet and went humbly to meet death, obedient to the end to His Father's will.

Jesus' example teaches all who love Him and strive to follow Him to pray as He prayed.

Jesus Taught to Change People's Hearts

In His teachings, Jesus did not aim to compel sterile intellectual assent. He wanted to change the hearts of His listeners—"to make a bad man good, and good man better," as President Brigham Young said (*Discourses of Brigham Young,* 449). Some of His most sublime yet most wintery teachings are found in the Sermon on the Mount. "Love your enemies, bless them that curse you, do good to them that hate you, and pray for them which despitefully use you, and persecute you." "Whosoever shall smite thee on thy right cheek, turn to him the other also. And if any man will sue thee at the law, and take away thy coat, let him have thy cloke also. . . . Give to him that asketh thee, and from him that would borrow of thee turn not thou away" (Matthew 5:44, 39–42).

Those sayings were hard for Jesus' listeners to accept, and they have not become easier over the centuries. But He knew that if we are ever to break the age-old cycles of hatred, racism, and bigotry that plague the human family, if ever blood-feuds and violence are to end, we must learn to change our hearts. That is what He expects of us: to become new creatures, with new hearts and new spirits (see Ezekiel 18:31), and no more disposition to sin. He will settle for nothing less.

C. S. Lewis, who saw so many things "as they really are," described the Savior's position on this matter as follows: "Christ says 'Give me All. I don't want so much of your time and so much of your money and so much of your work: I want You. I have not come to torment your natural self, but to kill it. No half-measures are any good. I don't want to cut off a branch here and a branch there, I want to have the whole tree down. I don't want to drill the tooth, or crown it, or stop it, but to have it out. Hand over the whole natural self, all the desires which you think innocent as well as the ones you think wicked—the whole outfit. I will give you a new self instead. In fact, I will give you Myself: my own will shall become yours'" (*Mere Christianity*, 165).

Jesus knows that it is not how much we talk about Him or profess belief in Him that determines who we really are. Rather, as a man "thinketh in his heart, so is he" (Proverbs 23:7). Jesus taught, "He that hath my commandments, and keepeth them, he it is that loveth me" (John 14:21). After all the verbal expressions of love and devotion are given, after all the preaching and exhortations are finished, we show what we really think of Christ by the way we keep His commandments. It's just that simple.

Jesus, when He taught about the Samaritan who helped a man beaten, robbed, and left for dead (see Luke 10:30–37), recited to His apostles and disciples the parable of the sower (see Matthew 13:3–9), or rebuked Simon the Pharisee for his self-righteous rejection of a woman with an unsavory past (see Luke 7:40–47), was reaching out to touch the hearts of His listeners. He called upon them, as He calls upon us, to be loving, merciful, kind, and forgiving— to give away our sins, change our hearts, refrain from unrighteous judgment of others, and come to Him. I repeat: He is the perfect Exemplar, not only by what He taught, but by His sublime example.

Jesus Taught and Blessed "the One"

Though He often spoke to large numbers of people, Jesus always reached out to the individual. Recall the story of the woman with "an issue of blood" who, in the midst of a crowd, hoping to be cured, reached out to touch the border of the Savior's garment. When Jesus perceived her faithful action and asked who had touched Him, she came, trembling, and declared "before all the people for what cause she had touched him." Jesus responded to her by saying, "Daughter, be of good comfort: thy faith hath made thee whole" (Luke 8:43–48).

Surrounded though He was by a multitude of people, Jesus was sensitive to and willing to focus on the needs of "the one."

Other powerful examples of Jesus' concern for the individual are found in the Book of Mormon. Just one of many: When the resurrected Jesus appeared before the faithful Nephite remnant, He invited them to come forth "one by one" to thrust their hands into His side and feel the prints of the nails in His hands and feet. Then they "did know of a surety and did bear record" (3 Nephi 11:15). Providing that opportunity took time, but it was important that each individual receive a personal witness of the resurrected Christ, who had conquered death.

"Come and see," and as you learn of Him and model your life after His, your ability to teach eternal truths, by word and example, will increase geometrically. I promise you that.

CHAPTER SIX

COME AND SEE . . . THE GRIEVING, ATONING MAN OF SORROWS

Behold the great Redeemer die,
A broken law to satisfy.
He dies a sacrifice for sin,
He dies a sacrifice for sin,
That man may live and glory win.
HYMNS, NO. 191

Jesus endured much suffering and disappointment during His mortal life. Not for nothing did Isaiah refer to Him as one who is "despised and rejected of men; a man of sorrows, and acquainted with grief: and we hid as it were *our* faces from him; he was despised, and we esteemed him not. Surely he hath borne our griefs, and carried our sorrows" (Isaiah 53:3–4). Similar sentiments were expressed by other prophets who foretold His mortality and messianic mission.

Jesus' sorrow was never directed at Himself. There was no self-pity in Him, no self-indulgence, no cry of "poor little me." What makes His sorrows so heartbreaking for those who love Him is that they were caused by the actions of others: by sin and pride, by the wrong-headed disdain and denial of the truth, and by the arrogant rejection of the glory of the sinless perfect One, who came to earth "to suffer, bleed, and die for man" (*Hymns,* No. 195). Through it all, however, Jesus remained totally steadfast to the cause to which He had been called. Ever loyal to His Father, ever giving all glory to Him, Jesus' love for the children of men, even those who rejected Him, never wavered. In the sublime fullness of His condescension, Jesus recognized that those who railed against Him and His message were in the main to be pitied.

It is characteristic of Him that He refused to defend Himself against the false accusations spewed out against Him at the bitter mockery of His so-called trial. "I gave my back to the smiters, and my cheeks to them that plucked off the hair: I hid not my face from shame and spitting" (Isaiah 50:6).

Though His body was beaten and broken, He endured without complaint the pain and humiliation inflicted upon Him. When asked by the high priest about His disciples and doctrine, Jesus replied simply, "I spake openly to the world. Ask them which heard me, . . . they know what I have said."

One of the officers struck Jesus, saying, "Answereth thou the high priest so?" Jesus replied with calm dignity and impeccable logic, "If I have spoken evil, bear witness of the evil: but if well, why smitest thou me?" (John 18:19–23). To the Roman procurator's query "What hast thou done?" Jesus deigned only to reply: "My kingdom is not of this world" (see John 18:33–36).

Most telling of all, perhaps, is that while He hung in agony on the cross, between two thieves, Jesus said of the Roman soldiers who had so sorely abused and tortured Him, "Father, forgive them; for they know not what they do" (Luke 23:34). What a sublime example of love and forgiveness! Jesus simply refused to hate. So, too, must we.

The prophet Joseph Smith, who endured more than his share of abuse, extended Christlike forgiveness to those who had wronged him. Daniel Tyler witnessed the actions of some members of the Church in Missouri, whose faith had been weakened by persecution. Repentant and contrite, some of them wished to return to full fellowship. Tyler recalled:

"One scene . . . was particularly touching, and showed the goodness of the [Prophet's] heart. A man who had stood high in the Church while in Far West, was taken down with chills or ague and fever. While his mind as well as body was weak, disaffected parties soured his mind and persuaded him to leave the Saints and go with them. He gave some testimony against the Prophet. While the Saints were settling in Commerce, having recovered from his illness, he removed from Missouri to Quincy, Illinois. There he went to work chopping cordwood to obtain means to take himself and family to Nauvoo, and a present to the injured man of God if, peradventure, he would forgive and permit him to return to the fold as a private member. He felt that there was salvation nowhere else for him and if that was denied him all was lost as far as he was concerned. He started with a sorrowful heart and downcast look.

"While on the way the Lord told Brother Joseph he was coming. The Prophet looked out of the window and saw him coming up the street. As soon as he turned to open the gate the Prophet sprang up from his chair and ran and met him in the yard, exclaiming 'O Brother, how glad I am to see you!' He caught him around the neck, and both wept like children. Suffice it to say that proper restitution was made and the fallen man again entered the Church by the door, received his Priesthood again, went upon several important missions, gathered with the Saints in Zion and died in full faith" (*Juvenile Instructor,* 15 Aug. 1892, 491).

THE PAIN OF LONELINESS

Jesus endured the bitter pains of loneliness throughout His ministry. When rejected by His listeners in the synagogue of Nazareth, Jesus proclaimed, in sorrow, "a prophet is not without honour, but in his own country, and among his own kin, and in his own house" (Mark 6:4). Who can fail to resonate to the pathos in His lament, "The foxes have holes, and the birds of the air have nests; but the Son of man hath not where to lay His head" (Matthew 8:20). It is apparent that during the three years of His mortal ministry, Jesus was without a permanent dwelling place. Not for Him were the comforts of home and hearth, of spouse and children. "I am become a stranger unto my brethren, and an alien unto my mother's children" (Psalm 69:8). By the end of His ministry, the apostles truly were Jesus' friends (see John 15:15), but the scriptural accounts make it clear that early on they did not understand fully who He was and whose errand He was on. How Jesus must have longed for the simple joys of friendship, the sweet unspoken understandings, the mutual forbearance that characterizes the relationships between true comrades. But that was not to be, and probably could not be, because of who He was.

THE PAIN OF REJECTION

Over and over again, Jesus experienced the sorrow of rejection resulting from misunderstanding. Few there were who understood the import of His message. All but a few were hard-pressed to believe He was who He claimed to be. As opposition mounted to His mission, the faith of many wavered, and "they walked no more" with Him.

The faith of many believers in Christ is at times sorely tried. Our spiritual foundations are battered by the ambiguities and apparent injustices of life. When such occurs, we find our only unassailable resting place, the Rock of our Salvation, in the sure and certain spiritual experiences of the past. It is the memory of those times when we have felt the Spirit, and know that God knows we have felt it, that sustains us. With Job we proclaim, "I know that my redeemer liveth" (Job 19:25), and that knowledge conveys all the faith needed to hang on, to endure in our unbelief until it is changed to belief, in the sure and certain knowledge that He will reveal more of Himself to us as needs be. "For he will unveil his face unto you, and it shall be in his own time, and in his own way, and according to his own will" (D&C 88:68).

Though as a group the Twelve remained faithful, Jesus knew that one of them would betray Him; one was evil, like unto his malignant master, who had fallen from highest height to the bottom of the pit of evil. Long before actually betraying Christ, Judas's apostasy had already begun in his blackened heart. Jesus knew from the beginning of His ministry where it would lead. Yet he shrank not from it.

Some there were who rejected Jesus because they simply didn't understand Him. Others, however, rejected Him because of malice or weakness. Away with Him, crucify Him, was their cry. No doubt the brutal executioner, who drove nails through Jesus' palms, wrists, and feet with the same callous disregard for suffering as shown by his Nazi counterparts during the Holocaust nearly two millennia later, was in that category. So, too, was the thief crucified alongside of Jesus, who "railed on him, saying, if thou be Christ, save thyself and us" (Luke 23:39). Most assuredly, however, the penitent malefactor who said unto Jesus, "Lord, remember me when thou comest into thy kingdom," received a different reward. In his heart were the stirrings of faith and repentance. "To day shalt thou be with me in paradise," Jesus said to him (Luke 23:42–43).

For much of Jesus' ministry, the leaders of the

Jews thirsted after His blood, hatching plot after plot to have Jesus apprehended and put to death. Though they posed as custodians of the law, the children of Abraham and Moses, they were in fact as whited sepulchres, full of dead men's bones and the stench of corruption, condemned by their own hypocrisy and arrogance (see Matthew 23:27). And they deeply resented being reminded of their true natures.

Members of the Sanhedrin knew full well that there was a growing belief among many of the common people that Jesus was indeed the long sought-after Messiah. Further extension of that belief would, they reasoned, cause a tumult among the people. And then the Romans, who hated disorder, would further restrict Jewish privileges. The only way to silence this miracle worker was to kill Him. That, at least, was the excuse used by the Jewish leaders (see John 11:47–53). Whether they knew it or not, they were functioning as the devil's agents in this sordid affair.

MODERN REJECTION OF JESUS

It does little good to argue over who was responsible for Jesus' death. What was done is done. It is, however, much more useful to ask whether He would be so treated today. Would (and do) people in our day reject Him as in days of old? Jesus Himself has provided the answer. In a revelation given to the prophet Joseph Smith in 1831, Jesus introduced Himself as "Him who is from all eternity to all eternity, the great I AM, even Jesus Christ. . . . He that receiveth my gospel receiveth me; and he that receiveth not my gospel receiveth not me" (D&C 39:1, 5). There it is, in a nutshell: whoever rejects Christ's gospel rejects Him. In rejecting the message they reject the Man. Acceptance of the gospel reveals whether or not a man accepts Jesus as Lord and Savior. If men reject the one, and hence the other, and if the animosity attending the rejection is sufficiently sour and bitter, it may well result in calls to trample Him underfoot and "judge him to be a thing of naught" (1 Nephi 19:9).

The Church of Jesus Christ of Latter-day Saints proclaims boldly that Jesus has revealed Himself anew and restored to the world the fulness of the everlasting gospel. Some accept that gladsome message, and in doing so accept Him who proclaims

Himself to be "the great I AM, Alpha and Omega, the beginning and the end, . . . which knoweth all things" (D&C 38:1–2). Others reject His message and turn their backs on Him. Many there are who love "darkness rather than light, because their deeds [are] evil" (John 3:19). They shall have their reward.

THE PAIN OF AFFLICTIONS

The prophet Isaiah noted that the Messiah, whom he did not live to see in the flesh, would bear the afflictions of His people: "In all their affliction he was afflicted, and the angel of his presence saved them: in his love and in his pity he redeemed them; and he bare them, and carried them all the days of old" (Isaiah 63:9). The witness of the Nephite prophets corroborates the biblical prophecies. King Benjamin, who received the information from "an angel from God," stated that He (Jesus) "shall suffer temptations, and pain of body, hunger, thirst, and fatigue, even more than man can suffer, except it be unto death; for behold, blood cometh from every pore, so great shall be his anguish for the wickedness and the abominations of his people" (Mosiah 3:7).

And the great Alma added his testimony: "He shall go forth, suffering pains and afflictions and temptations of every kind; and this that the word [i.e., the prophecy of Isaiah] might be fulfilled which saith he will take upon him the pains and the sicknesses of his people" (Alma 7:11).

In recounting these prophecies that Jesus would suffer pains and afflictions, it must be kept in mind that the Jesus of whom we speak is as He was when He dwelt among the children of men. Here, in mortality, Jesus was thirsty, hungry, and tired; here He ate, slept, laughed, and cried. Here He was bound by the limitations of a mortal body and earthly existence. In His glorified and exalted state as the resurrected living Lord, King of Kings, and Lord of Lords, Jesus is not subject to such limitations. Nor was He, of course, before He came to earth. But He condescended to make Himself subject to the rules—the limitations and promises, if you will—of mortality.

THE PAIN OF TEMPTATION

It may seem strange to even think for a moment that Jesus, a God, could be tempted, enticed to do that which is wrong. But temptation is an essential part of earthly probation, and Jesus was no exception. If we are to progress it "must needs be, that there is an opposition in all things" (2 Nephi 2:11). Jesus, who of course did not succumb to temptation, serves as the exemplar for us all, for though "He suffered temptations [He] gave no heed unto them" (D&C 20:22). He points the way for us, giving us strength from His example to overcome our own temptations. "For in that he himself hath suffered being tempted, he is able to succour them that are tempted" (Hebrews 2:18).

Matthew recorded the temptations Christ endured just prior to the beginning of His mortal ministry (see Matthew 4:1–11). Although Matthew's account in the King James version of the Bible indicates Jesus went into the wilderness to be tempted, the Joseph Smith Translation of Matthew 4:1 indicates He went to be with God. Righteous men do not seek temptation.

In the wilderness, weakened physically by forty days of fasting, Jesus met the devil, who, knowing of His hunger, invited Him to appease His appetite by turning stones to bread. Jesus demurred, answering, "Man shall not live by bread alone, but by every word that proceedeth out of the mouth of God" (Matthew 4:4). Then the Spirit transported Jesus to the pinnacle of the temple. (The account in the King James version of Matthew errs in stating it was the devil who transported Jesus; the Joseph Smith Translation sets the matter straight.) There the arch-tempter, appealing to what he hoped was Jesus' pride, vanity, and desire for public acclaim, called for a dramatic proof: "If thou be the Son of God, cast thyself down." Jesus replied: "Thou shalt not tempt the Lord thy God." The third temptation was perhaps the most seductive of all: From a high mountain the devil showed Jesus all the kingdoms and glory of the world. "All these things will I give thee, if thou wilt fall down and worship me." Jesus dismissed him: "Get thee hence, Satan: for it is written, Thou shalt worship the Lord thy God, and him only shalt thou serve" (Matthew 4:6–10).

The temptations He resisted typify the ways in which we, in our day, are seduced by the deceiver. As he did with Jesus, Satan plies us with invitations to indulge our physical appetites, satisfy our pride and vanity, and seek after the honors of men.

But, you may say, Jesus, after all, was a God. I'm just a poor, weak mortal. I can't withstand temptations as He did. To those who erroneously suppose that Jesus could not be tempted in the same way we mortals are tempted come these words of comfort: "For we have not an high priest which cannot be touched with the feeling of our infirmities; but was in all points tempted like as we are, yet without sin" (Hebrews 4:15). The Father's mercy is further evidenced by this declaration: "There hath no temptation taken you but such as is common to man: but God is faithful, who will not suffer you to be tempted above that ye are able; but will with the temptation also make a way to escape, that ye may be able to bear it" (1 Corinthians 10:13).

The Pain of the Crucifixion

Jesus suffered terribly at His crucifixion. His spiritual suffering defies human understanding, and will be discussed shortly, but His physical suffering, in and of itself, was so gruesome as to make one shudder in horror. Having first been beaten by His guards, Jesus was brutally flogged prior to His crucifixion. The scourging itself was almost enough to have put His life in serious jeopardy. That, indeed, was its intention. The usual instrument used in scourging was a short whip with several single or braided leather thongs in which small iron balls or sharp pieces of sheep bones were tied at intervals. The back, buttocks, and legs were flogged either by two soldiers who alternated their blows, or by one who alternated his positions. The blows, delivered overhand with all the force of a strong man, would have caused deep contusions, severe lacerations of the flesh, extensive blood loss, and excruciating pain. They undoubtedly left Jesus in severe shock. The fact that He was unable, because of physical weakness, to carry His cross to Golgotha indicates that the scourging Jesus received was particularly severe.

As was customary for those to be crucified, Jesus was required to carry His own cross—or at least the crossbar, which would have weighed between 75 and 125 pounds—from the flogging post to the site of His crucifixion. There He was nailed to the crossbar, using iron spikes, which, based upon archaeological evidence from a crucified body found in an ossuary near Jerusalem, were five to seven inches in length. The spikes were driven through His palms and then through His wrists; then the victim and crossbar were lifted onto the upright pole already in place and His feet were nailed to the pole. With the weight of His bloodied body being supported by the spikes, the excruciating physical agony on the cross can hardly be overstated.

Jesus died after a few hours, probably from shock and cardiorespiratory failure. The two thieves with Him had their legs broken to hasten death, but when the soldiers came to Jesus they did not break His legs, probably because He was already dead. (Note that in fulfillment of the prophecy in Exodus 12:46, the paschal lamb was not to have any of its bones broken.) One of the soldiers did pierce His side, probably with an infantry spear. The weapon, thrust between Jesus' right ribs, very likely perforated not only His right lung, but also His heart, thereby ensuring His death. (For a detailed description of the medical aspects of Jesus' death, see William D.

Edwards, et al, *Journal of the American Medical Association,* 1455–63).

The gruesome details of Christ's crucifixion underlie an important fact: He suffered intensely from the excruciating pain. But far greater was the spiritual pain resulting from the demands of the Atonement.

THE PAIN OF THE ATONEMENT

None of us who heard it will ever forget Elder Bruce R. McConkie's address at the April 1985 general conference of the Church. Rising from his sickbed, against the advice of his physician, he delivered a powerful discourse, made the more soul-stirring because his audience knew, as did he himself, that his mighty voice would soon be stilled in death. Speaking of the Savior, as he had so many times, Elder McConkie gave his own apostolic witness. Said he, "I am one of his witnesses, and in a coming day I shall feel the nail marks in his hands and in his feet and shall wet his feet with my tears. But I shall not know any better then than I know now that he is God's Almighty Son, that he is our

Savior and Redeemer, and that salvation comes in and through his atoning blood and in no other way" ("The Purifying Power of Gethsemane," *Ensign*, May 1985, 11). I wept, as did many others, to hear those stirring words, delivered by one who had spent so long as a special witness of Christ.

Knowing, as he surely did, that his conference address would be his last opportunity to speak to the Saints and provide them with counsel and advice, Elder McConkie chose to speak of what he termed "the most transcendent event that ever has or ever will occur, from creation's dawn through all the ages of a never-ending eternity." He spoke, of course, of the Atonement of Christ—that culminating glory of the most glorious of lives, which humbles us and drives us to our knees in gratitude and reverent worship of Him who died on Calvary's hill that we might live—and not only live but live again, under the most glorious of circumstances, with our Heavenly Father.

The Atonement is, at the same time, the most basic and fundamental doctrine of the gospel and perhaps the least understood of all the revealed truths. In a sense, it is beyond human comprehension. Try as we will, we cannot fully grasp it in all its majesty. We can at best comprehend only its broad outlines. The Atonement of Christ pays for our sins upon condition of our acceptance of Him and our obedience to His laws and ordinances. If we are not willing to accept those conditions, the full weight of divine justice must inevitably fall upon us. It cannot be otherwise. Christ, then, came to earth, as Elder McConkie summarized, to bring mercy to the repentant and justice to the unrepentant.

Christ's atoning sacrifice took place in a peaceful garden called Gethsemane. It still exists today, or at least a part of it does, nestled at the foot of the Mount of Olives. In Jesus' day, it was a quiet place where He and His apostles often went to pray and ponder. There the Savior offered Himself for the sins of the world. We cannot, any of us, fully comprehend what happened on that occasion. We know only that Jesus, in some way incomprehensible to the human mind, took upon Himself the sorrows, sins, and suffering of all of God's children. This was accomplished through great sacrifice, through untold agony. He sweat great gouts of blood from every pore. There is no pain He did not suffer nor anguish He did not know. But let Him describe it as He spoke through the prophet Joseph Smith to Martin Harris:

"Therefore I command you to repent—repent, lest I smite you by the rod of my mouth, and by my wrath, and by my anger, and your sufferings be sore—how sore you know not, how exquisite you know not, yea, how hard to bear you know not. For behold, I, God, have suffered these things for all, that they might not suffer if they would repent; but if they would not repent they must suffer even as I; which suffering caused myself, even God, the greatest of all, to tremble because of pain, and to bleed at every pore, and to suffer both body and spirit— and would that I might not drink the bitter cup, and shrink—nevertheless, glory be to the Father, and I partook and finished my preparations unto the children of men. Wherefore, I command you again to repent, lest I humble you with my almighty power; and that you confess your sins, lest you suffer these punishments of which I have spoken, of which in the smallest, yea, even in the least degree you have tasted at the time I withdrew my Spirit" (D&C 19:15–20).

How great was His agony, suffered for us; how infinite His love; how deep our debt. Then, having gone through this terrible ordeal, Jesus went to the sordid mockery of His trial. Accused, cursed, mocked, beaten, spit upon, crowned with a crown of thorns, scourged, he was taken to the hill of Calvary—there to be nailed to a cross between two malefactors. Wounded for our transgressions, bruised for our iniquities, held in derision and scorn, He hung in suffering on the cruel cross. During that time, in addition to the searing agony of the crucifixion itself, it is apparent that all of the exquisite pain and suffering Jesus experienced in Gethsemane recurred and was amplified beyond mortal capacity to endure. Even nature seemed to recoil in horror at the immensity of the event. Darkness filled the land.

Finally, His atoning sacrifice complete, His victory won—only then did Jesus say, "It is finished" and voluntarily give up the ghost.

Who among us, having contemplated Jesus'

suffering in Gethsemane and on the cross, as He atoned for the sins of all of God's children, could do other than echo these inspired words:

> I stand all amazed at the love Jesus offers me,
> Confused at the grace that so fully he proffers
> me.
> I tremble to know that for me he was crucified,
> That for me, a sinner, he suffered, he bled and
> died.
> Oh, it is wonderful that he should care for me
> Enough to die for me!
>
> HYMNS, NO. 193

WHAT DOES IT ALL MEAN?

What does Jesus' pain and suffering mean for me, as I struggle through the thickets of mortality? First of all, His sufferings and temptations are incomparably greater than mine. I can teach Him nothing about suffering. He sets His trials before us as a standard to guide our behavior. As Jesus obtained perfection through suffering, so too must we if we are to become as He is. There is no other way.

Secondly, as part of our schooling in mortality,

our faith will be tried by suffering. To those who remain faithful, the trials of our faith will "be found unto praise and honour and glory at the appearing of Jesus Christ" (1 Peter 1:7).

We are to bear our suffering with patience and forbearance as Jesus did. "When he was reviled, [he] reviled not again; when he suffered, he threatened not; but committed himself to him that judgeth righteously" (1 Peter 2:23).

When we suffer, from loneliness, rejection, affliction, or temptation, we can turn to Him for solace and relief. He will wrap us about in the cloak of His redeeming love. He will strengthen us, calm our fears, and give us the sure and certain hope that better days lie ahead, whether on this side of the veil or the other. "I can do all things through Christ which strengtheneth me" (Philippians 4:13).

There may be times we will suffer just because we are Christians. When such occurs, these inspired words of Peter bring solace and understanding: "For this is thankworthy, if a man for conscience toward God endure grief, suffering wrongfully. For what glory is it, if, when ye be buffeted for your faults, ye shall take it patiently? but if, when ye do well, and suffer for it, ye take it patiently, this is acceptable with God" (1 Peter 2:19–20). In other words, if you suffer as a Christian, be patient and humble, as Christ Himself was, and God will bless you.

"Come and see," and as you find Him, your tears will flow—tears of sorrow for His pain and your own complicity in its causation, and tears of gratitude for His glorious gift to all.

The grieving atoning man of sorrows, who "came to earth to suffer, bleed, and die for man," became, through His Atonement and Resurrection, the glorified, living Lord, the King of Kings, who will come again to earth. That is the central promise of the Christian gospel.

CHAPTER SEVEN

COME AND SEE . . . THE RISEN, LIVING LORD

He is risen! He is risen!
Tell it out with joyful voice.
He has burst his three days' prison;
Let the whole wide earth rejoice.
Death is conquered, man is free.
Christ has won the victory.

HYMNS, NO. 199

THE CHRIST OF THE EMPTY SEPULCHRE

After His death on the cross, the lifeless body of Jesus was delivered, at Pilate's direction, to Joseph of Arimathea, a secret disciple of Christ. Joseph was evidently a man of considerable position and influence and probably a member of the Jewish Sanhedrin. A "good man, and a just" (Luke 23:50), he had not consented to the sentence condemning

Jesus to death. Joseph was assisted in his somber task of taking Jesus' broken and lifeless body down from the bloodstained cross and preparing it for burial. His assistant was another member of the Sanhedrin, Nicodemus, he who had come to Jesus secretly by night (see chapter three). The two men cleansed the body, which would have been soiled with blood and sweat, wrapped it in clean linen and a large quantity of embalming spices, and placed it in a new sepulchre. The tomb, hewn as a sort of cave out of the rock, was located in a nearby garden, owned by Joseph of Arimathea.

All of this was done before sunset on the day Jesus was killed, before the beginning of the Jewish sabbath. (How ironic it is that those who had no compunctions about killing Jesus were adamant that He should not desecrate the sabbath by hanging on the cross on that day!) The door to the tomb was closed by rolling a great stone across it. The stone, more than likely, was perhaps 6 to 8 feet in diameter and 1 to 2 feet thick. It was placed in a trenchlike groove running parallel to the front of the tomb. The groove would have sloped downward, so the stone could readily be rolled into place. To roll the stone away, however, would have been much more difficult, since it would have to be rolled up an incline.

The chief priests and Pharisees, remembering Jesus' assertion that He would rise from the dead, and fearful of what would happen if His body were secreted away by His followers, demanded of Pilate that an armed guard of Roman soldiers be placed to keep watch over the sepulchre. With Pilate's consent this was done, and silence descended on the melancholy scene, save, we can be sure, for the ribald conversation of the soldiers.

Early on the first Easter Sunday, while it was still dark, the earth began to quake. An angel of the Lord, Matthew records, "descended from heaven, and came and rolled back the stone from the door, and sat upon it. His countenance was like lightning, and his raiment white as snow" (Matthew 28:2–3). The guards, displaying none of the vaunted discipline of Roman soldiers, fled in terror. No matter, they had nothing left to guard. The tomb was empty, its occupant gone.

Although the writers of the Gospels are in

general agreement in their recounting of the events that occurred that glorious first Easter morn, the experience of Mary Magdalene, recounted in detail only in chapter 20 of John's gospel, is worthy of special mention.

Following her discovery of the disappearance of the Lord's body, Mary stood outside the sepulchre, weeping, her heart broken at the loss of her beloved friend. Stooping down, she looked into the empty tomb and saw two angels sitting there, one at the head and the other at the feet, where the body of Jesus had lain.

"Woman, why weepest thou?" they asked.

The grieving woman replied through her tears: "Because they have taken away my Lord, and I know not where they have laid him" (John 20:13). She thought only in terms of human grave robbers, or others who had desecrated the tomb of her Master, not of God's miracle. At that point, such was beyond her comprehension.

Then she became aware that another personage stood nearby. Supposing, in her agony of spirit, that he was the caretaker of the garden, she, still weeping, implored, "Sir, if thou have borne him hence, tell me where thou has laid him, and I will take him away" (John 20:15).

What pathos, what sorrow Mary's words convey! Hers had been a hard life. Jesus had at one time cast seven devils out of her (see Mark 16:9). Though she has been imagined by some to have been unchaste, perhaps even a prostitute, there is no scriptural evidence warranting the slanderous assertion. However, it is reasonable to assume that before Jesus came into her life, fear, misery, rage, and depression had been her daily lot. All of that had been changed as He cast out the devils that had enslaved and tormented her, and brought peace and joy to her heart. And now perhaps the only true happiness Mary had ever known was gone, crucified on Calvary's cruel cross. Is it any wonder she wept, perhaps recalling not only her own sense of personal loss but also the misery and torment of her life before she met Jesus?

He who stood before her spake but one word. "Mary," He said. In an instant she knew it was Jesus Himself who spoke. Darkest despair turned at once into almost incomprehensible joy. Overwhelmed by the rush of emotion that flooded through her, Mary reached instinctively to embrace Him, uttering the endearment "Rabboni," meaning "my Beloved Master."

Jesus gently forbade her. "Touch me not," he said, "for I am not yet ascended to my Father: but go to my brethren, and say unto them, I ascend unto my Father, and your Father; and to my God, and your God" (John 20:16–17). There was now, in Jesus' resurrected and immortalized state, a divine dignity and majesty about Him, which did not permit close personal familiarity. He who had condescended to become man was now God. It is apparent also that at this time Jesus had not yet ascended to His Father and reported to Him.

We can but imagine that glorious reporting scene: Father, I have done all Thou didst command me to do. I have drunk out of that bitter cup Thou didst give me. I have glorified Thee in taking upon me the sins of the world. I have suffered Thy will in all things (see 3 Nephi 11:11). To which, perhaps, came the divine reply: Well done, my Beloved Son.

In Thee I am well pleased. In Thee I have glorified my name. Welcome home.

Nor can we but imagine Mary's bittersweet joy as she hurried to Jerusalem to carry out the sacred errand given to her by her beloved Master. She must have longed to stay with Him, in the sweet comfort of His beloved presence. But what ecstatic joy must have hurried her feet on their sacred journey. He *lives!* He *lives!* We have not lost Him after all! And what radiance must have shown in her face as she burst into the room where the sorrowing disciples sat. I have seen the Lord, she proclaimed (see John 20:18). Nothing would ever be the same again. Not for Mary, not for the disciples, and not for all the world. Praise be to the Father: "Christ the Lord is ris'n today . . . love's redeeming work is done . . . Jesus' agony is o'er . . . Darkness veils the earth no more" (*Hymns*, no. 200).

JESUS IS SEEN BY MANY

Although Mary Magdalene was the first mortal of whom we have record to see the risen Savior, she was soon joined by others. Mary, the mother of Joses

(Joseph) and of James the younger; Salome, the mother of the apostles James and John; and other faithful women came to the empty sepulchre after Mary Magdalene had been there and departed. They too saw angels who, witnessing their perplexity and confusion, asked, "Why seek ye the living among the dead? He is not here, but is risen" (Luke 24:5–6). As the women were hurrying back to Jerusalem to tell the disciples what they had heard and seen, Jesus Himself appeared to them. He greeted them, saying, "All hail." And they fell at His feet, worshipping Him. But they were still frightened, perhaps still confused at having seen the unseeable. "Be not afraid," said Jesus in reassurance, "go tell my brethren that they go into Galilee, and there shall they see me" (Matthew 28:9–10).

Luke probably heard the account from eyewitnesses, perhaps even from the mother of Jesus. He records that the women returned from the sepulchre and told all these things to the apostles and others. But their testimony was too fantastic and seemed to the apostles "as idle tales, and they believed them not" (Luke 24:11).

Why were the women not believed? Would we, in the supposedly enlightened twenty-first century, have responded any differently? Would we have had the simple faith to believe that the Savior had indeed risen from the dead, as He, Himself, had said He would? Or would we have demanded proof; would we have concluded that the women were hysterical or mistaken or driven from rationality by their overwhelming grief? Most of us, I fear, would not have believed. We would not have been consumed by the ineffable joy that fills the bosom of one who is a witness of the living Savior.

There are many reasons for such skepticism, the most prominent of which, perhaps, is that the ancient apostles, like us, were human. The great universal human experience is death. Everyone we know—our parents, grandparents, and, if we live long enough, our adult friends—will all die. Eventually, of course, each of us will die. There are no exceptions. To think otherwise is to think the unthinkable.

So it is understandable that the apostles did not at first believe that Jesus had indeed risen from the dead. It is true they had seen life restored to the son of the widow of Nain (see Luke 7:11–15); to the daughter of Jairus, the ruler of a synagogue (see Mark 5:35–43); and to Jesus' beloved friend Lazarus (see John 11:43–44). But in each case that had been a restoration to mortal life that would one day be terminated permanently. They had heard Jesus proclaim Himself as the Resurrection and the Life. "He that believeth in me, though he were dead, yet shall he live: And whosoever liveth and believeth in me shall never die" (John 11:25–26). But they had failed to understand the literal truth of the Savior's words. What had happened to Jesus was qualitatively different from all other human experience. It was a resurrection—a raising the dead, not to complete a mortal life and then die, but to live forever. It set the pattern for all. "For as in Adam all die, even so in Christ shall all be made alive" (1 Corinthians 15:22).

That same Easter Sunday, two disciples, Cleopas and another (possibly Luke, since he recorded the event), were walking from Jerusalem to a nearby village called Emmaus. The distance is about eight miles. Of course, there was only one thought on their minds—the strange story the women had told of an empty sepulchre and angels who said "Jesus is not here. He is alive. He has risen."

As they walked along, deep in conversation, they were joined by another traveler. He seemed in all respects to be just another wayfarer. Nothing about his dress, demeanor, or speech gave them a clue to his real identity. It was Jesus Himself, "but their eyes were holden that they should not know him" (Luke 24:16). As they walked and talked, Jesus asked them why they seemed sad and disturbed. Cleopas, perhaps a little exasperated by this stranger who seemed to know nothing about the momentous events of the past week, told him about Jesus, the mighty prophet who had been crucified at the instigation of the chief priests and the rulers. Then he mentioned the strange story of the women who had astonished the disciples by their insistence that Jesus was alive.

Jesus chided them: "O fools, and slow of heart to believe . . . ought not Christ to have suffered these things, and to enter into his glory?" Then He "expounded unto them in all the scriptures the things concerning himself" (Luke 24:25–26, 27).

They came to the village of Emmaus and still unaware of the stranger's identity, the two disciples invited their fellow traveler to spend the night with them. As they sat to share a meal together, He took bread and blessed and brake it. Then, in an instant, they knew who He was. Perhaps there was something in His voice, or maybe they saw His wounded hands and wrists. In any event, they recognized Him as the resurrected Lord. He vanished out of their sight. They rose from the table, no doubt astonished, perhaps chagrined, at their own inability to see Him in His true identity. Then they recalled: "Did not our heart burn within us, while he talked with us by the way, and while he opened to us the scriptures?" (Luke 24:32). With joy they quickly made their way back to Jerusalem to report the event to the apostles.

Cleopas and his companion found the apostles and a few other disciples meeting in secret behind closed doors "for fear of the Jews" (John 20:19). The two travelers were greeted with a joyful announcement that "the Lord is risen indeed, and hath appeared to Simon," and they shared their own experience with the resurrected Lord (see Luke 24:34).

We know nothing of that meeting of Jesus with Simon Peter, but we can imagine Peter, shamefaced and deeply repentant, having denied Christ thrice, falling to his knees before the Master. Perhaps Peter felt that through his lack of courage he had forfeited his place in the kingdom. Jesus, we can be sure, greeted Peter with loving forgiveness, reassuring him that Peter still would be called upon to wear out his life as the chief apostle. It seems reasonable to assume that Jesus may have both instructed and strengthened Peter for the onerous task that lay ahead, that of leading the infant Church.

While the little group of believers communed together in nascent faith and understanding, Jesus Himself appeared before them. Luke says they were "terrified and affrighted, and supposed they had seen a spirit," but He showed them His wounded hands and feet, inviting them to "handle me, and see; for a spirit hath not flesh and bones, as ye see me have" (Luke 24:39). Their joy was full, yet still they dared not believe: what they were seeing and hearing was just too good to be true, too wondrous to be real. To further demonstrate His reality He asked for food and ate it before them. Then were the eyes of their understanding opened. He was no ghost, no spirit from another realm, but a living, glorified Man. "Praise God, it *is* true! He lives, He lives!" they must have said to themselves.

Before Jesus left He conferred upon each of those present the Holy Ghost and gave to the apostles the power to remit or retain sins (see John 20:22–23; it must, however, be noted that the Holy Ghost sent by Jesus from the Father did not come in person until the Day of Pentecost. The First Presidency's statement of 5 Feb. 1916 [see *Deseret News* of that day] makes that point clear). Well did Jesus know the turbulent trials that lay before the little band of faithful servants.

Jesus appeared to many others during His forty-day ministry between His resurrection and ascension. One week after His resurrection, that is on the following Christian sabbath, Jesus appeared again to the assembled disciples. They were meeting once more behind closed and presumably locked doors. This time Thomas, an apostle who had been absent from the meeting a week before, was present.

Thomas was a rationalist. He could scarcely have doubted that the tomb was indeed empty. Jesus was no longer there. But the stories that He had actually been seen, very much alive after having been just as obviously dead, were just too much for Thomas to accept. "Except I shall see in his hands the print of the nails, and put my finger into the print of the nails, and thrust my hand into his side, I will not believe," Thomas declared (John 20:25). We should be careful not to judge Thomas too harshly. After all, stories about dead men coming to life aren't all that easy to believe!

It was in this setting that Jesus appeared to Thomas and the others. He invited Thomas to touch Him, to see for himself that Jesus indeed had a resurrected body of flesh and bones. "Reach hither thy finger, and behold my hands; and reach hither thy hand, and thrust it into my side: and be not faithless, but believing." Thomas did so, and his disbelief was turned at once to unquestioning acceptance. "My Lord and my God," he exclaimed in reverent worship (John 20:27–28).

Jesus' gentle chiding of Thomas served to remind

him—and all of us—that belief based on faith is more admirable than belief based on experience. Those who expect all religious truth to be proven experientially before they will believe ask for too much. It is more blessed to walk by faith through life, secure in the knowledge that God will reveal what we need to know, line upon line and precept upon precept.

On other occasions, Jesus appeared to Peter and six other apostles at the Sea of Galilee (see John 21); to the eleven apostles on a mountain in Galilee (see Matthew 28:16); to more than 500 brethren at once, probably in Galilee (see 1 Corinthians 15:6); to James (see 1 Corinthians 15:7); and to the eleven apostles at the time of His ascension from a place near Bethany (see Mark 16:19; Luke 24:50–51). In addition, after His ascension, He was seen by Paul on the Damascus Road (see Acts 9:4–5) and previously by Stephen (see Acts 7:56).

Soon after the resurrected Jesus had ascended in Judea He visited the Americas. There, lived other sheep of whom He had spoken (see John 10:16; 3 Nephi 15:21). His death at Jerusalem had been signaled to the people living in the western hemisphere by terrible natural calamities. Earthquakes, lightning, fire, depressions of the earth, the inrush of the sea, and other catastrophic events resulted in many cities being utterly destroyed. Great loss of life occurred. Then thick darkness fell—a darkness so oppressive that the dazed survivors could not even light a fire or a candle. The constellation of disasters has been explained by some as being compatible with a major volcanic eruption. Be that as it may, the terrified remnant who had survived the devastation bemoaned their fate. "O that we had repented before this great and terrible day, . . . then would our mothers and our fair daughters, and our children have been spared. . . . And thus were the howlings of the people great and terrible" (3 Nephi 8:25).

Following these catastrophic events, a voice was heard in the darkness, proclaiming the destruction of the wicked. The people fell silent. It was the voice of Jesus. He pled with the people to come unto Him and be saved. "O all ye that are spared . . . will ye not now return unto me, and repent of your sins, and be converted, that I may heal you?" (3 Nephi 9:13).

There was silence in the land, broken only after many hours by the voice of Jesus, again calling upon the people to repent and promising to gather His people as a hen gathereth her young.

The morning of the third day, the darkness dispersed, and the survivors could see for themselves the destruction surrounding them. It became apparent that those who had been spared were the more righteous—those who had "received the prophets and stoned them not; and . . . had not shed the blood of the saints" (3 Nephi 10:12).

About six weeks later, the surviving Nephites, penitent, contrite, and still in awe at what had happened to their society, were gathered at the temple in the land called Bountiful. Their thoughts were constantly on Jesus, whose death in far-off Jerusalem had been signaled by the great calamities that had torn Nephite society apart and led to such destruction and loss of life.

Again a voice was heard: "Behold my Beloved Son, in whom I am well pleased, in whom I have glorified my name—hear ye him" (3 Nephi 11:7). As they gazed upward, the people beheld a man, clothed in a white robe, who descended out of heaven. He came and stood in the midst of them. The people thought it was an angel who had come, but then the personage spoke: "Behold, I am Jesus Christ, whom the prophets testified shall come into the world. And behold, I am the light and the life of the world; and I have drunk out of that bitter cup which the Father hath given me, and have glorified the Father in taking upon me the sins of the world, in the which I have suffered the will of the Father in all things from the beginning" (3 Nephi 11:10–11).

At these words the people fell to the earth in humble adoration, remembering that their prophets had prophesied many years before His coming that Jesus would show Himself unto them. "Come forth," said Jesus, "that ye may thrust your hands into my side, and also that ye may feel the prints of the nails in my hands and in my feet, that ye may know that I am the God of Israel, and the God of the whole earth, and have been slain for the sins of the world" (3 Nephi 11:14). The people did as He had directed. Then in an ecstasy of joy, with one accord, they cried, "Hosanna! Blessed be the name of the Most

High God!" (3 Nephi 11:17). And they fell at Jesus' feet in adoring reverence.

Jesus ministered on successive days and at considerable length among the Nephites. He preached the gospel to them, organized His Church bearing His name, taught the correct mode of baptism and the ordinance of the sacrament, called and authorized twelve disciples to carry out the work of the ministry, healed the sick, and blessed the Nephite children. Then, His work done, His Church established, He departed to His Father. We can be certain that Jesus knew the Nephite church, after a period of righteousness, would revert to its old, sinful ways and destroy itself in a welter of blood and horror. He must have wept over that knowledge.

DOUBTS AND DENIALS

Jesus had scarcely risen from the dead before there were those who denied the reality of this greatest of happenings in all of history. Within the day, bribe money had been given to shut the mouths of the soldiers assigned to ensure Christ's tomb remained sealed. The soldiers were instructed by the chief priests to "say . . . his disciples came by night, and stole him away while we slept. . . . So they [the soldiers] took the money, and did as they were taught" (Matthew 28:11–15).

Major doctrinal disputes regarding the resurrection wracked the Christian church for four centuries after Christ's death. Much of First Corinthians centers on the Apostle Paul's testimony of the reality of a physical resurrection. Several malignant heresies made deep inroads into Christian thought in the centuries after Jesus' birth. They include the docetic heresy. The term *docetic* is derived from the Greek word *dokio,* meaning "to seem to be." The Docetics taught that Christ, during his mortal life, had only a phantasmal body and not a real one. Christ only appeared to be the man Jesus. Docetics taught that the physical body Christ displayed after the resurrection was only an illusion. According to Docetic thinking, for Christ to have had contact with the material world would have "soiled" Him and defiled His divine nature. What ridiculous nonsense!

The Apostle John wrote First and Second John, at least in part, to warn of and combat false notions about the resurrection of Jesus. For instance: "And every spirit that confesseth not that Jesus Christ is come in the flesh is not of God: and this is that spirit of antichrist, whereof ye have heard that it should come; and even now already is it in the world" (1 John 4:3). Further, "Many deceivers are entered into the world, who confess not that Jesus Christ is come in the flesh. This is a deceiver and an antichrist" (2 John 1:7).

Cerinthus, a first-century A.D. heretic, gave his name to another bizarre theory which deals with the resurrection. The Cerinthian heresy taught that the spirit that inhabited Jesus' mortal body descended into the man Jesus at the time of his baptism and departed just prior to his suffering on the cross. According to Cerinthus's fanciful thinking, Christ did not die for our sins; it was only the man Jesus who died on the cross.

To further confuse the issue, the Council of Chalcedon (A.D. 451) declared that Christ must have two natures—one human, which suffered on the cross, and the other divine, which felt nothing. Most modern Christians are unaware of this pernicious nonsense, but there it stands, as evidence of how far from the truth the post-apostolic church had wandered. Is it any wonder why Latter-day Saints simply cannot accept the hellenized Christ of the creeds and councils?

Is there no end to the litany of error that characterizes our faithless age? In a recent highly publicized book, A. N. Wilson, formerly a lecturer in theology, no less, at Oxford University, speaks of Jesus' resurrection as a "whopping lie." He suggests that the post-Calvary man who appeared to so many was in reality James, "the brother of the Lord" (*Jesus: A Life*, 60).

Another monstrous falsehood, promulgated by those who deny the Christ, is that Jesus did not die on the cross, but was taken down, resuscitated, and spirited away by His followers. Barbara Thiering, an Australian academic, has promoted the nonsense that Jesus lived on after Calvary and went with Paul on his missionary travels. She even claims that Jesus (having divorced the first) met His second wife at Philippi during these travels (see *Jesus and the Riddle of the Dead Sea Scrolls*).

Although most of the spurious drivel in our day denying the reality of Jesus' resurrection comes from misguided clerics and academics, more learned than they are wise, substantial numbers of "ordinary" members of mainline Christian churches also do not believe in Christ's life and resurrection. In a survey conducted in 1985, nearly three-fourths of the clergy of the Church of England professed a belief in the resurrection, but only 52 percent of the lay members believed in the bodily resurrection of Jesus (*Emerging Trends* 7:1, Jan. 1985). For many of the honorable men and women of the world, including increasing numbers of those who call themselves Christian, Christ's resurrection and longed-for return to earth to reign as King of Kings and Lord of Lords is not something to be taken literally. His unique role as the Atoning Living Lord receives increasingly less attention. Yet as Paul said: "If Christ be not risen, then is our preaching vain, and your faith is also vain. . . . If in this life only we have hope in Christ, we are of all men most miserable" (1 Corinthians 15:14, 19).

Where do the Latter-day Saints stand on this

matter? Our position is simple. It is scriptural. It is clear. We believe with all our hearts that the biblical and Nephite records are literal truth. Jesus died, rose again in glory as a resurrected being, and will come again to the earth in a glorious future time. The prophet Joseph Smith summarized the Latter-day Saint position on the resurrection succinctly as follows: "So that after the testimony of the Scriptures on this point, the assurance is given by the Holy Ghost, bearing witness to those who obey Him, that Christ Himself has assuredly risen from the dead; and if He has risen from the dead, He will, by His power, bring all men to stand before Him" (*History of the Church*, 2:19).

We rest our case

"Come and see"—and raise your voice with millions of other believers, in praise of Him who conquered death, won victory over the grave, and became the triumphant King of Kings.

CHAPTER EIGHT

COME AND SEE . . . THE TRIUMPHANT KING OF KINGS

I wonder, when he comes again,
Will herald angels sing?
Will earth be white with drifted snow,
Or will the world know spring?
I wonder if one star will shine
Far brighter than the rest;
Will daylight stay the whole night through?
Will song birds leave their nests?
I'm sure he'll call his little ones
To gather round his knee,
Because he said in days gone by,
"Suffer them to come to me."

CHILDREN'S SONGBOOK, 82–83

JESUS' FINAL INSTRUCTIONS TO HIS APOSTLES

As His forty-day ministry following the resurrection came to an end, Jesus led the eleven faithful apostles out of Jerusalem, "as far as to Bethany" (Luke 24:50), and blessed them. He counseled them to remain in Jerusalem, to await an endowment of "power from on high" (Luke 24:49). "Wait," said He, "for the promise of the Father, which . . . ye have heard of me. For John truly baptized with water; but ye shall be baptized with the Holy Ghost not many days hence" (Acts 1:4–5). How the apostles, and all members of the infant Church, would need that power! Jesus, of course, fully understood the trials through which the Church and its leaders would have to make their way. ("And ye shall be hated of all men for my name's sake," [Matthew 10:22; see also John 15:19]).

To the apostles He gave a special charge, one in stark contrast to their earlier commission. When they were first called and sent out, Jesus had instructed the Twelve to "go not into the way of the Gentiles, [nor] into any city of the Samaritans . . . but go rather to the lost sheep of the house of Israel" (Matthew 10:5–6). That commission now had changed. The gospel of Christ was to be taken to all the world, to every nation, kindred, tongue, and people. "Go ye into all the world," Jesus said, "and preach the gospel to every creature. He that believeth and is baptized shall be saved; but he that believeth not shall be damned" (Mark 16:15–16). The apostles' preparatory schooling was over: salvation was to be offered to all of God's children, everywhere. Through faith in Christ, followed by repentance and baptism, *all* were to be given the opportunity to "come unto Christ, and be perfected in him." To all those who love God with all their might, mind, and strength, His grace suffices, "after all we can do" (2 Nephi 25:23), and by that grace "ye may be perfect in Christ" (Moroni 10:32).

In their original charge, the Twelve had been authorized and instructed to declare that "the kingdom of heaven is at hand" (Matthew 10:7). They misunderstood, thinking that Jesus was referring to an earthly kingdom—one of power and might. They thought in terms of Solomon's glory, of the "pomp and circumstance" of the world. Jesus knew otherwise. He had stood, after a dark, hate-filled night of insult and abuse, before Pontius Pilate, the Roman procurator. Pilate, quickly discerning this was no ordinary mortal who stood before him, submissive yet majestic, inquired, "Art thou the King of the Jews?"

Jesus answered, "My kingdom is not of this world: if my kingdom were of this world, then would my servants fight, that I should not be delivered to the Jews: but now is my kingdom not from hence." Pilate continued his questioning. He, too, could think of kings and kingdoms only in terms of the power and pomp displayed by imperial Rome, his master. "Art thou a king then?" Jesus answered with calm dignity: "Thou sayest that I am a king. To this end was I born, and for this cause came I into the world, that I should bear witness unto the truth" (John 18:33–37). Jesus knew *exactly* who He was and *is,* and who He was and is *not.* His kingdom was not of this world, nor will it be when He returns. His kingdom was, is, and ever will be in stark opposition to the kingdoms of the world.

But, as they conversed together for the last time, the eleven still did not fully understand. "Lord," they asked, "wilt thou at this time restore again the kingdom to Israel?" In other words, "Wilt thou remove the Roman yoke from our necks and give us back not only our political independence but, even more, the glory days when we were really *something* in this world? When can we expect, what is, after all, only our just due as the chosen people: the power to make our enemies tremble and all men acknowledge we are rulers of all we survey?"

Jesus gently chided them: "It is not for you to know the times or the seasons, which the Father hath put in his own power. But [and note the promise given again] ye shall receive power, after that the Holy Ghost is come upon you: and ye shall be witnesses unto me both in Jerusalem, and in all Judaea, and in Samaria, and unto the uttermost part of the earth" (Acts 1:6–8).

Jesus does not wish us to worry about earthly power. He has more important work for us to do, in all the world. Our responsibility is to be witnesses for Him, to bring people unto Him, that they might know Him, and the Father who sent Him. And He will endow us with the power needed to accomplish that task. That is His solemn promise. The Holy Ghost will give us that power, and with it we can accomplish something grander and greater than all the kingdoms of the world could ever offer.

Jesus' understanding of the ephemeral impermanence of the kingdoms of the world brings to mind the words of the poet Shelley, who in his poem "Ozymandias," wrote of a traveler in a far and distant land who came upon an awe-inspiring scene:

Two vast and trunkless legs of stone
Stand in the desert. Near them, on the sand,
Half sunk, a shattered visage lies, whose frown,
And wrinkled lip, and sneer of cold command,
Tell that its sculptor well those passions read
Which yet survive, stamped on these lifeless
        things,
The hand that mocked them, and the heart that
        fed:
And on the pedestal these words appear:
"My name is Ozymandias, king of kings:
Look on my works, ye Mighty, and despair!"
Nothing beside remains. Round the decay
Of that colossal wreck, boundless and bare
The lone and level sands stretch far away.

JESUS' ASCENSION

The scriptural account of the ascension and the events surrounding it continues: "And when he had spoken these things, while they beheld, he was taken up; and a cloud received him out of their sight. And while they looked steadfastly toward heaven as he went up, behold, two men stood by them in white apparel; which also said, Ye men of Galilee, why stand ye gazing up into heaven? this same Jesus, which is taken up from you into heaven, shall so come in like manner as ye have seen him go into heaven" (Acts 1:9–11).

He was gone! The sky toward which they gazed was empty. The Light and Life of the world had left them. Though some Christian commentators portray the eleven as being "dumfounded, like children who have lost their parents" (e.g., Phillip Yancey, *The Jesus I Never Knew*, 226), the scriptures recount otherwise. Luke records that the eleven worshipfully and "with great joy" returned to Jerusalem, there to await the promised coming of the Comforter (see Luke 24:52).

That is not to say, however, that joy and sorrow cannot be in close juxtaposition within the same individual. Jesus underlined that truth with remarks He made at the Last Supper. It must have been a somber affair, heightened by the grandeur of His teachings, but tinged with deep sorrow because it finally dawned on the apostles that Jesus would not long be with them, and that one of their number was a traitor. "I go to prepare a place for you. . . . I will come again, and receive you unto myself," He said (John 14:2–3). "A little while, and ye shall not see me: and again, a little while, and ye shall see me, because I go to the Father" (John 16:16). The apostles, still not fully understanding, remarked, "What is this that he saith unto us?" (John 16:17).

Perhaps they had at last begun to feel the chill of His impending death, but did not yet comprehend His glorious resurrection. The Christ of the empty tomb still was a stranger to them. Jesus spoke in power and plainness, patiently reiterating His teachings. His separation from His beloved friends would be brief, and sorrow quickly would be swallowed up in joy. "Ye shall weep and lament, but the world shall rejoice: and ye shall be sorrowful, but your sorrow shall be turned into joy. A woman when she is in travail hath sorrow, because her hour is come: but as soon as she is delivered of the child, she remembereth no more the anguish, for joy that a man is born into the world. And ye now therefore have sorrow: but I will see you again, and your heart shall rejoice, and your joy no man taketh from you" (John 16:20–22).

In other words, His apostles would sorrow at His death, feel the stirrings of hope and joy as they began to understand the meaning of the empty tomb, but feel an effulgent outpouring of joy as they came to realize both the reality and the promise of His Atonement and Resurrection. The Apostle Paul, who felt that same surge of joy, put it thusly: "Death is swallowed up in victory. O death, where is thy sting? O grave, where is thy victory? . . . thanks be to God, which giveth us the victory through our Lord Jesus Christ" (1 Corinthians 15:54–55, 57).

WHY DID JESUS LEAVE US?

It is clear that Jesus knew of His departure from the very beginning. In His great intercessory prayer, He pled with the Father: "And now, O Father, glorify thou me with thine own self with the glory which I had with thee before the world was" (John 17:5). He was planning to go home again, to beloved celestial halls, to reassume the glory that was His. He had set it aside, voluntarily, to come to earth, "to walk upon his footstool and be like man, almost" (*Hymns*, no. 175). But His purpose had always been to fulfill His mortal mission—to carry out His errand as the atoning, redeeming Savior—and then to return to His Father. The mission of carrying on His work would be delegated to others. They would have to carry His message of love and hope to all the world.

But why didn't He just stay on earth and demonstrate the power of His glory to every nation, kindred, tongue, and people? Who would have dared gainsay Him, when confronted with conclusive proof of the reality of His sovereignty? Wouldn't my own struggles be made infinitely easier if I could sit, literally at His feet, and hear His beloved voice, and gain strength and insight and wisdom from just being with Him?

The answer to these questions must be no. As hard as it may seem sometimes, the demands of agency aside, our spiritual advancement actually is enhanced, not hindered, by Jesus' leaving. He

Himself knew that, of course. "It is expedient [i.e., beneficial, advantageous] for you that I go away: for if I go not away, the Comforter will not come unto you; but if I depart, I will send him unto you" (John 16:7). Jesus' promise was clear. He will not leave us to our own often feeble resources. "The Comforter, which is the Holy Ghost, whom the Father will send in my name, he shall teach you all things, and bring all things to your remembrance, whatsoever I have said unto you" (John 14:26). "When the Comforter is come," He said, "even the Spirit of truth, . . . he shall testify of me" (John 15:26). We were not therefore to be left bereft of help. The Holy Ghost would testify of Christ. Furthermore, Jesus, speaking of His apostles, noted, "Ye also shall bear witness, because ye have been with me from the beginning" (John 15:27).

From Jesus' departure onward, Peter and his associates, strengthened by the Spirit beyond their mortal capacities, would wear out their lives in bearing witness before the world that Jesus is the Christ. How pleased Jesus must have been when Peter, "filled with the Holy Ghost" (Acts 4:8), stood before the rulers, elders, and scribes and boldly proclaimed Jesus' divine role as the Atoning Savior: "There is none other name under heaven given among men, whereby we must be saved" (Acts 4:12).

Finally, Jesus understood that in His absence we show our love for Him by the service we give to others. In every land, there is so much misery and hardship, so many tears, so much sorrow. Mother Teresa, the wonderful Catholic nun who wore out her life serving with loving compassion the wretched, degraded, and rejected castoffs of the Calcutta slums, felt that those she served were Christ Himself, "in a most distressing disguise." In her view, as she and her companions cared for the poor and the dying, "It is the hungry Christ we are feeding, it is the naked Christ that we are clothing, it is the homeless Christ that we are giving shelter" (David Aikman, *Great Souls, Six Who Have Changed the Century*, 221).

I have the deepest respect for Mother Teresa, whose compassion for the poor was both compelling and sublime. But her argument is overblown and not correct, albeit symbolically striking. I cannot accept her idea that the poor *literally* become Christ in disguise, just as I reject with respect (and for the same reasons) the Catholic doctrine of transubstantiation—the belief that the sacramental bread and wine (or water) *literally* become the blood and flesh of Christ.

Divergent Christian views on this matter have their roots in different understandings of the last parable Jesus gave. It was delivered shortly before He suffered in Gethsemane, was betrayed, condemned to die, and crucified. It is the parable of the sheep and the goats, found in Matthew 25:31–46. I do not think it was by chance that Jesus waited until so late in His ministry to give the counsel contained therein. He knew that His time was short. He would soon be leaving, and there still were many lessons to be taught the Twelve. In light of the shortage of time, He had to concentrate only on those matters of greatest importance. Furthermore, His teachings had to be such that the principles presented readily would be understood and accepted. Jesus could not leave until His followers learned that we are to aid the poor, the hungry, the naked, the homeless *in remembrance of Him,* treating them as we would treat Him were He with us in the flesh. When He returns "in his glory, and all the holy angels with him" (Matthew 25:31), all people, everywhere, will be judged by the extent to which they have given aid and succor to those in need *in His absence,* in remembrance of Him. He made the reason clear: "Inasmuch as ye have done it unto one of the least of these my brethren, ye have done it unto me" (Matthew 25:40).

WHEN WILL JESUS RETURN?

Jesus was in Jerusalem to attend the passover feast. The last Sunday of His mortal ministry, He entered the city in triumph (see Matthew 21:8–9), borne on the back of a donkey, to the acclaim of a great multitude, and in fulfillment of prophecy (see Zechariah 9:9). In the course of His last walk from Jerusalem to Bethany, where He customarily stayed (at the home of Mary, Martha, and Lazarus), Jesus rested on the Mount of Olives. To at least Peter, James, John, and Andrew, and probably to all of the apostles, He proclaimed the imminent destruction of the temple.

"When shall these things be?" they asked, "and what shall be the sign of thy coming, and of the end of the world?" (Matthew 24:3). We can infer from the close proximity of the two questions that His interlocutors understood the destruction of the temple would be separate from and precede the events relating to His Second Coming and "the end of the world." Jesus spoke at length about the calamities that will precede His Second Coming. In answering their inquiry as to when the Second Coming will occur, He both revealed and concealed. As He often did, Jesus resorted to a parable, using as His teaching tool the fig trees that grew on the Mount of Olives.

"Now learn a parable of the fig tree; when her branch is yet tender, and putteth forth leaves, ye know that summer is near: so ye in like manner, when ye shall see these things come to pass, know that it is nigh, even at the doors." (This sign applies with equal force to both the impending fall of Jerusalem and to events immediately preceding His Second Coming.) He continued: "But of that day and that hour knoweth no man, no, not the angels which are in heaven, neither the Son, but the Father. Take ye heed, watch and pray: for ye know not when the time is" (Mark 13:28–29, 32–33). In sum, no one knows the day or the hour of His coming. But faithful disciples will know how to read the signs and portents of things that shall occur before the great and dreadful day of the Lord comes. Watch, be vigilant and prepare. But do not fear!

WHAT SIGNS WILL PRECEDE HIS COMING?

It is not my intention in this book to outline in detail the numerous signs of the times that will precede His coming. That has been done, masterfully, by others. Suffice it to say, in general terms, that the long-anticipated day of the Lord's coming will represent the effulgent fruition of the hopes and longings of God's prophets from the beginning of time. Nor should it be forgotten that His Second Coming flows directly from His first. The two are inextricably linked, and the connection between them is the glorious Atonement. Jesus came to earth, "made himself of no reputation, and took upon him the form of a servant" (Philippians 2:7) and ransomed all of God's children from temporal death. In the indescribable agony of the Atonement, in Gethesmane and on Golgotha, He bore the sins of all on conditions of repentance. His Second Coming will represent His final triumph over the world of evil. The cosmic struggle between light and darkness will be ended. Satan will be bound and the wicked destroyed. Righteousness will sweep over the earth as the waters cover the mighty deep. In that day, as Isaiah prophesied, "The wolf also shall dwell with the lamb, and the leopard shall lie down with the kid; and the calf and the young lion and the fatling together. . . . they shall not hurt nor destroy in all my holy mountain" (Isaiah 11:6, 9). "Then the eyes of the blind shall be opened, and the ears of the deaf shall be unstopped. Then shall the lame man leap as an hart, and the tongue of the dumb sing: for in the wilderness shall waters break out, and streams in the desert. And the parched ground shall become a pool, and the thirsty land springs of water" (Isaiah 35:5–7).

A recurring, underlying theme in any consideration of the events preceding the Second Coming is the growing dark stain of evil, which envelops the world like a black shroud. Its malignant roots lie in the poisoned soil of rejection of Christ and His gospel. The natural man—carnal, sensual, and devilish—rejects God and His Son. He demands blood, revenge, retribution; his memory of wrongs, real or imagined, never dims; he sees compassion as weakness and holds forgiveness in contempt. The humble meekness of Christ is not for him: he prefers the swaggering braggadocio of the brazen covenant-breaker who mocks at sacred things.

In addition to the generalized climate of wickedness that pervades the world, and perhaps not unrelated to it, is the growing weakness and increasing irrelevancy of large segments of so-called mainline Christianity. An expanding gulf separates the Latter-day Saints from other Christians. In saying so I have no wish to "blow our own horn." The Lord knows the Latter-day Saints have many faults, and of *all* peoples perhaps least live up to their responsibilities. That said, however, we aver that the Christian church lost its way soon after the original apostles (with the notable exception of John the Revelator;

see D&C 7) had sealed their testimonies with their blood. I take no pleasure from that affirmation of an apostasy from Christ's gospel. For all its faults and errors the Christian church has blessed the lives of untold millions. It has brought hope, joy, and comfort to countless hearts. It kept the lamp of civilization lit for centuries. In every age and in every land humble folk, both rich and poor, have acknowledged Christ as Lord and Savior and have served Him as best they knew Him, practicing charity and forgiveness to others. All Christian churches preach, teach, and practice a measure of the truth. The goodness of so many of their members puts me to shame.

Yet, simply put, in the years after the death of the New Testament apostles, the Church suffered a loss of divine authority, as philosophers and theologians diluted the simple truths of Christ's gospel with pagan philosophical systems. As the Church drank the heady wine of politics and power and blurred what should be a clear distinction between the things of God and the things of Caesar, it lost its way. The apostasy—for that is what it was—already had begun to corrode and erode the foundations of the Church within less than two decades of Christ's death. In nearly every letter written by the Apostle Paul to the struggling branches of the Church throughout Asia Minor, we read of his deep concerns that all was not well. Indeed it was not. A dark night of spiritual darkness settled over the earth, broken only by the light of Christ, which lighteth every man who cometh into the world (see John 1:9; Moroni 7:18–19; D&C 93:2).

Lacking the fullness of the gospel to guide the people, bereft as it is of the voices of apostles and prophets, is it any wonder wickedness abounds in the world? We can expect the clouds of spiritual darkness to deepen and grow more noxious until they are first dissipated and then destroyed by the brightness of His coming.

As part of the generalized moral corruption of the last days, Jesus prophesied that "there shall arise false Christs, and false prophets, [who] shall shew great signs and wonders; insomuch that, if it were possible, they shall deceive the very elect" (Matthew 24:24). What is meant by false Christs? In that lamentable category we would include false preachers, false doctrine, and false ways of worship, which substitute the philosophies of men, given a veneer of spirituality by being intermingled with scripture, for the simple truths Jesus taught. Such actions lack divine approval or authorization.

Speaking of conditions in our time, the great Nephite prophet Moroni recounted yet another associated prophecy of the last days: false churches—churches "that shall say: Come unto me, and for your money you shall be forgiven of your sins" (Mormon 8:32). Moroni lamented, "O ye wicked and perverse and stiffnecked people, why have ye built up churches unto yourselves to get gain? Why have ye transfigured the holy word of God, that ye might bring damnation upon your souls? . . . I speak unto you as if ye were present, and yet ye are not. But behold, Jesus Christ hath shown you unto me, and I know your doing" (Mormon 8:33, 35).

Apostasy and corruption of sacred truths, if they are to be corrected, require a revelatory restoration of all things. That such would occur had indeed been foreseen by John, who "saw another angel fly in the midst of heaven, having the everlasting gospel to preach unto them that dwell on the earth, and to every nation, and kindred, and tongue, and people. Saying with a loud voice, Fear God, and give glory to him; for the hour of his judgment is come" (Revelation 14:6–7). We proclaim that the glorious First Vision, wherein the prophet Joseph Smith saw the Father and Son, ushered in the dispensation of the fulness of times. Moroni and other heavenly beings restored all things, including priesthood authority and keys, required for the governance of the Lord's earthly kingdom.

It seems almost paradoxical that one of the signs of the last days is that, in the midst of growing wickedness and spiritual darkness, the Lord's Church will be established in the nations of the world. Not only is His Church, The Church of Jesus Christ of Latter-day Saints, established worldwide, it is thriving and growing rapidly. We have our challenges, to be sure, but the work of building the kingdom moves on apace. How grateful I am for the guidance and instruction provided by living prophets. They are legal administrators in the Lord's cause. Without their steadying hands at the tiller, I fear we would soon be in deep water and deep trouble.

Though, as indicated, we do not know the date of the Second Coming, we do know for certain that the gospel must be preached in all nations before the Lord returns. He himself said so: "And this gospel of the kingdom shall be preached in all the world for a witness unto all nations; *and then shall the end come*" (Matthew 24:14; emphasis added). Though we now have 60,000 missionaries in the field, roughly speaking, it is apparent we still have much to do before we have fulfilled our mission to preach the gospel to all the world. But it must be done: All people must hear the warning voice, so they can prepare for the coming of the Son of Man, who will wreak judgment on the wicked and ungodly.

WHAT ARE WE TO DO IN THE MEANTIME?

The answer is simple. "Come and see," and I promise you will find Him. Then, be patient. He will come when He comes. In the meantime, wear out your life in service to Him, treating others in remembrance of Him, as you would were each of them Jesus Himself. Be not weary in well-doing.

Replace the selfishness and carnal sensuality of the natural man with the humble altruism of the man of Christ. Look forward with joy and anticipation to the day of His coming and so live your life that when He does come He will say to you, "Well done, thou good and faithful servant" (Matthew 25:21). Sing in your heart and in your congregations the song of longing anticipation:

> Come, O thou King of Kings!
> We've waited long for thee,
> With healing in thy wings
> To set thy people free.
> Come, thou desire of nations, come;
> Let Israel now be gathered home.
>
> Come, make an end to sin
> And cleanse the earth by fire,
> And righteousness bring in,
> That Saints may tune the lyre
> With songs of joy, a happier strain,
> To welcome in thy peaceful reign.

HYMNS, NO. 59

Epilogue

It is now two millennia since the Prince of Peace was born in Bethlehem of Judea. Empires have come and gone, each enjoying its short day in the sun and then, in turn, slipping away into the mists of time. Tyrants with bloody hands have hacked and butchered their way across the world's stage for a season, until they too have gone the way of all flesh. Men and women of talent and genius in the arts and sciences have adorned their day and bequeathed priceless legacies of truth and beauty to succeeding generations. Captains of industry and government have made their marks for all to see. But above and beyond them all, changeless and eternal, stands the lone figure of one man, Jesus Christ, the Redeeming Savior of the world, the Only Begotten Son of the Father, the Holy One of Israel.

His gift of immortality for all and eternal life for the faithful banishes the ancient enemies of death and oblivion, replacing them with a bright fulness of hope.

His message of love, mercy, and forgiveness displaces the carnal sensuality of the natural man, setting a new and exalted standard for human behavior.

His insistence that all men and women everywhere are brothers and sisters, that "all are alike unto God" (2 Nephi 26:33), rejects for all time old prejudices and tribal hatreds, replacing them with love and acceptance.

His call to all to forsake and repent of their sins and come unto Him motivates millions to look deep into their own hearts and change their lives for the better.

His understanding that true leadership is based on service, not power or coercion, sets new standards for those who aspire to influence others.

His concern for the poor and needy, the oppressed and downtrodden, the widow and orphan, teaches all that charity, the pure love of Christ, is the highest and most exalted human motivation.

His rejection of the tawdry materialism, which enslaves our society, gives new purpose to life, replacing acquisition with giving and caring, as we learn to seek "first the kingdom of God and his righteousness" (3 Nephi 13:33).

Over the centuries, ever since angels proclaimed to sorrowing women, "He is not here, but is risen" (Luke 24:6), untold millions, of every nation, kindred, tongue, and people, have worshipped him as King of Kings and Lord of Lords, wearing out their lives in service to Him, as best they have understood Him.

All who come to Him with broken hearts and contrite spirits, who lay their burdens at His feet, who are willing to give away all their sins to know Him, will find Him and know that He is "the way, the truth, and the life: no man cometh unto the Father, but by [Him]" (John 14:6).

As I move ever deeper into the shadows of the autumn of mortality, I await with greater anticipation the joy of wetting His feet with my tears. In common with millions of others who love Him, these words of a centuries-old hymn ring daily in my heart:

Jesus, our only joy be thou,
As thou our prize wilt be;
Jesus, be thou our glory now,
And thru eternity.

HYMNS, NO. 141

Sources

Abrams, M. H., et al., eds. *The Norton Anthology of English Literature.* 5th ed. 2 vols. New York: W. W. Norton & Company, 1986.

Aikman, David. *Great Souls, Six Who Have Changed the Century.* Nashville: Word Publishing, 1998.

Anderson, Richard Lloyd. *Understanding Paul.* Salt Lake City: Deseret Book, 1983.

Ballard, Melvin R. *Melvin J. Ballard—Crusader for Righteousness.* Salt Lake City: Bookcraft, 1966.

Bronowski, Jacob. *The Ascent of Man.* Boston: Little, Brown and Company, 1973.

Children's Songbook. Salt Lake City: The Church of Jesus Christ of Latter-day Saints, 1989.

Clark, J. Reuben, Jr. Conference Report, April 1937, 22–27.

Edwards, William D., et al. "On the Physical Death of Jesus Christ." *Journal of the American Medical Association,* 21 March 1986, 1455–63.

Firmage, Edwin B., ed. *An Abundant Life: The Memories of Hugh B. Brown.* Salt Lake City: Signature Books, 1988.

Hinckley, Gordon B. "Save the Children." *Ensign,* November 1994, 52–54.

Hymns of The Church of Jesus Christ of Latter-day Saints. Salt Lake City: The Church of Jesus Christ of Latter-day Saints, 1985.

Kimball, Spencer W. *The Teachings of Spencer W. Kimball.* Edited by Edward L. Kimball. Salt Lake City: Bookcraft, 1982.

Lee, Harold B. *Decisions for Successful Living.* Salt Lake City: Deseret Book, 1974.

Lewis, C. S. *Mere Christianity.* Glasgow: William Collins and Sons, 1952.

McConkie, Bruce R. *Doctrinal New Testament Commentary.* 3 vols. Salt Lake City: Bookcraft, 1965–73.

———. "The Purifying Power of Gethsemane." *Ensign,* May 1985, 9–11.

McKay, David O. *Pathways to Happiness.* Salt Lake City: Bookcraft, 1957.

McKay, John P., et al. *A History of World Societies.* 5th ed. New York: Houghton Mifflin, 2000.

Ogden, D. Kelly, and R. Val Johnson. "All the Prophets Prophesied of Christ." *Ensign,* January 1994, 31–37.

Packer, Boyd K. *Teach Ye Diligently.* Salt Lake City: Deseret Book, 1975.

Sagan, Carl. *Cosmos.* New York: Random House, 1980.

Smith, Joseph. "Gift of the Holy Ghost." *Times and Seasons* 3:823–26.

———. *History of The Church of Jesus Christ of Latter-day Saints.* Edited by B. H. Roberts. 7 vols. Salt Lake City: The Church of Jesus Christ of Latter-day Saints, 1932–51.

———. *Teachings of the Prophet Joseph Smith.* Selected by Joseph Fielding Smith. Salt Lake City: Deseret Book, 1976.

Smith, Joseph Fielding. *Answers to Gospel Questions.* 5 vols. Salt Lake City: Deseret Book, 1957–66.

Tanner, N. Eldon. "Judge Not, That Ye Be Not Judged." *Ensign,* July 1972, 34–36.

Thiering, Barbara. *Jesus and the Riddle of the Dead Sea Scrolls.* San Francisco: HarperCollins, 1992.

Tyler, Daniel. "Recollections of the Prophet Joseph Smith." *Juvenile Instructor,* 15 August 1892, 491–92.

Valetta, Thomas. "The True Bread of Life." *Ensign,* March 1999, 6–13.

Whitney, Orson F. *Elias: An Epic of the Ages.* New York: Knickerbocker Press, 1904.

———. *Life of Heber C. Kimball.* Salt Lake City: Bookcraft, 1945.

Wilson, A. N. *Jesus: A Life.* New York: W. W. Norton, 1992.

Wordsworth, William. "Lines Composed a Few Miles above Tintern Abbey." In *The Norton Anthology of English Literature,* edited by M. H. Abrams, et al. 5th ed. 2 vols. New York: W. W. Norton & Company, 1986.

Sources

Yancey, Phillip. *The Jesus I Never Knew.* Grand Rapids: Zondervan, 1995.

Young, Brigham. *Discourses of Brigham Young.* Selected by John A. Widtsoe. Salt Lake City: Deseret Book, 1941.

INDEX